THE ROADMAP TO PURPOSE

A GUIDE FOR MEN WHO 'HAVE IT ALL'

DIMPLE THAKRAR

authors
AND CO.

Disclaimer - No Medical or Personal Advice

The information in this book, whether provided in hardcopy or digitally (together 'Material') is for general information purposes and nothing contained in it is, or is intended to be construed as advice. It does not take into account your individual health, medical, physical or emotional situation or needs. It is not a substitute for medical attention, treatment, examination, advice, treatment of existing conditions or diagnosis and is not intended to provide a clinical diagnosis nor take the place of proper medical advice from a fully qualified medical practitioner. You should, before you act or use any of this information, consider the appropriateness of this information having regard to your own personal situation and needs. You are responsible for consulting a suitable medical professional before using any of the information or materials contained in our Material or accessed through our website, before trying any treatment or taking any course of action that may directly or indirectly affect your health or well being.

CONTENTS

Foreword   7

1. What's the Point?   13
2. What is the Current Position?   29
3. Why Don't CEOs Lead in their Relationships?   39
4. The Life Stages of a Man   57
5. The Tunnel   84
6. The Entrepreneur   96
7. The Masculine and Feminine   110
8. Relationships and Communication   126
9. Why Do YOU Keep F**ing Up?   136
10. What Do Women Really Want?   149
11. Addiction to Pleasing   162
12. The Bonus - How to gain confidence with   175
    powerful women
13. So What Now?   183

DEDICATION

This book is dedicated to my beloved Atul Thakrar, a man who has not only chosen to walk this path of life with me every day, but cherishes the crazy lady inside of me. He chooses to evolve and grow with me every day.

I love you, Mr Thakrar. Thank you for choosing to be my man for over thirty years!

FOREWORD

We live in a dimension of thought. This is exhibited and demonstrated by everything you have already created. Your creations and your successes did not happen before the thought of them, therefore, the mind is the builder.

Whether you realize it or not, in every moment you are creating your reality, a reality that arises from both your conscious and your unconscious thoughts, behaviors, beliefs, actions, reactions, perceptions, ways of being, and so forth.

If you are reading this book, then when it comes to creating what appears to be success in the eyes of others, your conscious thoughts have clearly been a powerful ally. Whether you realize it or not, so too have your unconscious thoughts. However, while they may have served you in building success (perhaps because you were seeking external validation or importance), chances are likely they do not serve you well in your personal life or relationships.

There is no doubt your journey up to this point has been an exciting, profound roller coaster ride of ups and down, of expansions and contractions, of wins and losses, and of heartbreaks and despair. Despite however many peaks and valleys you've traversed, you would have to agree that in this process you have come to know yourself in greater degrees, therefore, all of these experiences—the good, the bad, and the ugly— have the potential to be of great value. But there is an even greater journey before you, and that is the journey to the unknown self.

This journey will require you to go deeper and farther than you have ever gone before, and it will require you to look at parts of yourself that you may not want to look at. But I assure you, if you are able to unearth the unconscious drivers of your life, you will liberate yourself from a past that has been lording over you—in many instances, without you even knowing it. In liberating yourself from your past, you can finally meet the you you've never met.

If you are willing to look deep within, you *will* find the answers you seek, and in that process of uncovering hidden strata of traumas and the protective behaviors that were born out of them, you will bring forth throughout your life sweeping new levels of success, and these successes will have nothing to do with fast cars and shiny objects. Because really

—what good are all the toys in the world if you are not happy with the person you see in the mirror every morning?

What's more, what good are all those material possessions if you can't share with someone your immaterial, authentic self? Those beautiful aspects of the soul which have aided you in your creations, as well as the ones that have held you back when they manifested as the ugly aspects of the unchecked ego—which unbeknownst to your former unknown self—was running the show.

At the end of your life you can't take your toys with you, and I can assure you they won't mean shit to you when you're lying on your death. All you can take with you is the love you created and the love you have shared, and your greatest legacy will not be about your wealth, fame, or riches, but about your love that endures.

This book is a calling to transform and awaken—to come into the right mind, right thought, and right action; to align the mind, body, and spirit (i.e., the energy that engenders and enlivens us) into oneness and wholeness. When you do this, new possibilities that were once never available to you will fall into your lap with ease and grace.

Now know that transformation is a never-ending process—not only because change is the natural state of nature—but because the self is an endless labyrinth of discovery. However, the more you discover with openness, curiosity, and non-judgement about the person looking back at you in the mirror, the more you will grow to love that person, and the more you grow to love that person, the greater the gifts your life will give back to you.

Now here's the thing. Time is a human construct. If you take away its perceived limitations, all you would be left with is the present moment. All of this is to say—there is no tomorrow when you engage in the process of transformation and human potential.

There is only one now.

So what are you waiting for? Your future self—a more evolved, more present, more patient, more loving, more generous, more awakened self—is calling you into greater levels of love, wholeness, and oneness.

Tim Shields (USA)

Editor, ghostwriter, and author of "A Curious Year in the Great Vivarium Experiment"

'A MAN WITHOUT
PURPOSE MAY AS
WELL BE DEAD.'

Tony Robbins

1

WHAT'S THE POINT?

T his book is for the man who has it all on paper. You know the guy I mean. You have the corner office, the homes in Europe, the Maldives, and London. You have been through the struggles of success and some failure in life and could write a book on it. What you have learnt in life is worth its weight in gold and you have a longing to pass this on, yet there is one piece of the jigsaw holding you back. This niggling thing deep in your soul that if you could just nail and control, life would be 'perfect', freeing and so complete.

In this book we are going to walk the roadmap to what that missing piece is and how you can discover it. The difference is that possibly for the first time in your life, you get to be in control. Now hear me out, I know what you are thinking. You're thinking, *I am in control of my life, I decide.*

The title is The Roadmap to PURPOSE and yet throughout the book you will find me talk a lot about women and relationships. Here is why, (first bomb here) most men feel a failure when their women is unhappy. It's at that moment that they switch their purpose from them to 'keep the wife happy.' This is the moment you hand your balls over and lose self respect and her respect. Understand that the methods I talk of will not only fix your relationships but put you back on track to YOUR purpose. Now that is how you reclaim your manhood and regain RESPECT..

I will explain what the missing jigsaw piece is. This is going to be so simple and obvious when I say it but will stop you in your tracks, because it's stating the obvious that shifts worlds. This piece of the jigsaw is 'the power of a woman.'

Why is it that you can run huge organisations with thousands of people and yet when it comes to that one woman, you know the one I mean, *the one*... They hold such power and make you make decisions that make no logical sense. If it was in a business setting you would never in a million years make that decision. In fact, they cost you a million each time you go there.

Once again, I am not going to tell you anything groundbreaking but only the truth. 'Love is blind' and so you find yourself making the same mistakes over and over again.

This book will not only give you the answer to this crazy dichotomy that you have relied on for most of your life but also a new roadmap. It's a map to your own unique road that possibly for the first time in your life you are going to be in control of. For the first time in your life a woman (me) is going to let you take full control of your roadmap to purpose, success and fulfilment in all areas of your life through gaining control of your relationships. This will result in you having such clarity on who you are and the man you are in your relationships.

Say goodbye to all the hangers-on and gold diggers and hello to a lifelong queen who respects, values and supports you as you do her. I know you feel that this is a huge problem and it is impossible to achieve but all I ask is that you keep an open mind. Are you prepared to hear me out? After all, what have you got to lose? The price of this book and your time in reading it?

If you are still with me then we have established rapport and I am very grateful for your curiosity. Let's get started.

In this book you will discover why you have everything on the outside - the money, success, the cars, the homes and the wives / girlfriends, the corner office; you have it all and yet you still feel lost. Like, what is the point of it all?

You might have some of these thoughts of disappointment/shame/betrayal:

'Why did I work so hard to get to this?'

'Was it all worth it?'

'I should feel successful but I don't; I feel lost.'

You might even feel like you are failing despite the outward signs of success. I mean, if you were on the outside of your life looking in you would be telling yourself, 'Get a grip, snap out of it. What's your problem?' You may even have friends who say this to you now or maybe this is the first time, as you are reading, you have become aware that, yes, this is exactly how you feel.

This is exactly the kind of man I work with. I have been married for 26 years to this kind of man and I have provided transformation for over two decades. I have come to realise that you can't change a problem if you aren't even aware it is a problem. Sometimes we need to state the obvious. We need to hear it and read it. The challenge for men, when you have identified the obvious, is how to put words to how that makes you 'feel.' Yes... the 'feelings' word.

I know most of you have avoided the 'feelings' word like the plague. It's not that you don't feel, it's that it can often be very painful because of past experiences with ex-wives, childhood experiences and so on. We don't need to unpack all that. I don't believe for the purposes of this book or for how I coach it actually helps to talk about the shit. You will discover I am very straight talking, so please don't be offended.

My focus is to identify the problem, fix it and move on. But in order to fix it we do have to tap into feelings. It is the cement that holds the blocks in the roadmap together. It's the cement that is holding together your current roadmap to the point you are at right now.

That's right, you already have a roadmap right now. It's a roadmap to 'feeling' unsuccessful and you are so tired of walking that same path. Picture an old man stooped over, with a heavy old overcoat, wearing the best, handcrafted Italian leather, bespoke shoes. He is walking that brick road and is weary. He is so sick of the end destination. Every time he reaches the end point he seeks the next road and starts walking along it, hoping it will lead somewhere different. The problem is that he keeps using the same materials, same cement, same bricks or blocks to build the same road.

The worst thing of all about this picture is that he keeps going round and round in circles leading to the same destination just in a different season and so it looks different on the way. He is so tired of going round and round in circles that he has reached the point where he doesn't want to feel any more - he wants to be numb and so he stops using cement, and the bricks fall and crack and he tries so hard to keep walking and building the road, a path that no one else dares to travel, until he takes a breath and just stops.

All sound familiar?

Unfortunately, many successful CEO executives never get off that road and each time they travel it, it gets more and more unstable and crumblier until one of two things happens - they die on it, literally or metaphorically, or they try a shiny new road which eventually leads to the same road. In other words, they try a new wife, new house, new life, which also ends in divorce, bitterness and exhaustion.

I know this picture is bleak. I won't lie and I know if you are reading this you can not only relate but you have probably been here for a long time.

I am here to tell you there is hope. This can change in weeks once you have the right raw materials and faith that there is another road and map. Quite frankly, I am so excited for you because you are the 1% of the elite that not only believe there is a new roadmap and want to seek it, but are prepared to do the work!

I have to challenge you in this book to get you to success, so I am giving you fair warning... but I don't believe you are afraid of this, right? In fact, I bet you expect to be challenged in life. You want to grow and you know that you're only expanding when you are stretched.

In this book I will take you on a journey to simply find your purpose and feel so full and happy in you that you start to become a magnet for only amazing people and opportunities. Before we go into the 'how' I want to explain how this book should be used. It is the most important part of this book and should not be skipped over and is the only time I will direct you on how to build your own roadmap.

This book is intended for you to design your own path with the paving blocks I provide you with. It is not intended for sheep but lions, leaders. Men who have all their lives done the things that everyone said were impossible and have taken the path to success that no other man dared to travel. This book is designed for men who lead themselves. I will provide the blocks for you to lay so you can design your own way. It is by no way written for me to spoon feed you or mother you. If that is your desire this is not the book for you. Please put it down because I guarantee you it will frustrate the hell out of you.

The way this book is to be used is like the children's adventure books; you know, the ones where you design your story and outcome. Unique to you, nobody telling you what, who, how or when to do it. The idea is that after this chapter you can choose to read each chapter in order or to dip in and out in whichever order you want. There is no wrong or right; remember, this is your unique roadmap. You are possibly wondering how on earth it will make any sense if you read it out of order. Ask yourself the question: when have you ever done anything by the 'rules'? In fact, aren't rules there to be broken? And that is what this is like. When you allow yourself to go with your gut instinct, that is when you will get the information you need at the exact time you need it. You are in the driver's seat on this one. Enjoy the ride.

Maybe this is the first time you are allowing yourself to be in charge of your relationship destiny and for some of you it may feel a tad scary or vulnerable. What if you get it wrong? What if you get hurt?

It is really important that at this stage you understand where that fear comes from so you can move past it. It's actually one of the first things I take my 8/9-figure earning clients through. Let's firstly identify how it shows up for you. 'I feel lost', 'I feel as though my manhood has been taken', 'I can't do wrong for doing right', perhaps? These are key sentences I hear over and over again.

The problem with feeling lost, particularly in relationships, is that you are lost because you have literally lost your 'manhood' and part of that is because you gave up the right to make your own decision in your relationship through fear. Fear of being rejected, abandoned or not loved. If you are feeling some resistance right now, that is good. Why? Think about all the times you felt resistance in your business life. How did you respond? Did you turn the other way? Or did you welcome the challenge? You welcomed the challenge, right? Why? Because over the years you have learnt to realise that success comes from facing your challenges, resulting in a feeling of overwhelming satisfaction. That is the name of the game to feel satisfied.

Here, then, lies the first point: when you feel that same resistance in your relationships, what is your response? Do you run in the other direction? Give in and lose yourself? Or do you face it? Be aware, that's all I ask at this stage. Notice your pattern.

Right, then, so the trigger or resistance is the start of any roadmap to success.

Understand that 'abandonment'. It doesn't have to be something major in your childhood. It can be as simple as you being raised in a single parent family or your father working long hours or being away a lot. Or he may have been physically present but not emotionally, repeating history as his father did with him and so on.

There is no right or wrong, no need to blame or shame and here is why. The blame and shame don't help you or them. It is like giving them poison and you choosing to drink it. Wanting them to pay for the shitty childhood leaves you angry and bitter. How is that working out for you so far? Pointless, right?

So let's get clear and recap:

1. Keep an open mind about new roadmaps that you haven't travelled yet.
2. Fear of being in control in relationships may have been the reason you have been held back.
3. The fear comes from childhood fears of lack and abandonment.

The next question that comes up is why you have kept this fear for so long and not got rid of this destructive behaviour. Firstly, you may have not even recognised it as fear and even now be resistant to acknowledging it. If that is the case please call it what you want but understand that we all have fear and it is a feeling that helps us expand and act. However, until we become aware if it

However, until we become aware of it we hold on to things that give us something. What has this fear given you? Let me explain in an analogy. Imagine the fear is fuel in your car. The car represents financial success. This fear has been the fuel for your success all your life. It's what has got you from a Mini to a Ferrari. The only problem is that the bigger and more horsepower the car has the more fuel it needs. So you create more fuel through fear. Now here is the problem with that. This type of fuel is limited because it is manmade; it is not provided by Mother Nature which has an endless supply.

And so when supplies run out from time to time your car stops working. It's not sustainable. You not only cap your success you also cap the enjoyment of the ride.

The only way you have an endless supply of fuel is to tap into Mother Nature's endless supply. I will tell you what that supply is later in the book, even though you are not going to like it.

Now we have established how to navigate the book and your fears, what I am about to reveal is not for everyone. In fact, it is only for the elite, top 1%. Which I believe you are. It's for those who want to be successful not only in their work but, most importantly, in life as well. It is for a man who is a high achiever and wants it all.

That's right, this book is not about work or life success, but BOTH. Love, life and living legacy. Yes, you can have it all!

Perhaps you are sceptical of this. Perhaps you don't believe that it's possible to be incredibly successful in both work and relationships. Maybe you believe that something has to suffer.

One of my clients would repeatedly say, 'There is no such thing as work-life balance; it's impossible.' And he would constantly utter sentences like, 'If people say they have work-life balance, they are lying.'

Now, this is a man who has two ex-wives and two ex-long-term girlfriends. He clearly - in the past - has manifested exactly what he says. And he would be right. He believed it was impossible and so for him, it was.

I know what you are thinking - what is the point of this book then? I know why you might think that, but here is the point; you will literally manifest what you think, say and believe.

The client I am referring to is a man who has taken seven companies to 8/9 figure exits but didn't believe it was possible to have a happy, successful relationship at the same time as running businesses. Surely then, there is no hope for the rest of you, right? But here is the thing...

He believed he would never fail in business so he didn't.

He believed that in order to succeed in business you have to fail in love. I know you might not like the word fail, but it is exactly that. High achievers, I am talking to you when I say you must stop fearing failure in love; learn from it, even learn to love it!

'You can't have both,' was this particular man's mantra and so that is exactly what happened.

The first point to highlight here is that you have to believe that work-life balance is possible for YOU. You can't run a race knowing you are going to lose. If that is the case, there is no point even bothering to get to the starting line, let alone attempting to step towards the finish line!

Pointless. Don't waste your time, energy and money. God knows, this mindset must have cost him millions and I am sure many of you reading this will know the figure all the exes have cost you both in dollars and heartache.

But if you have held those beliefs before then let this be the book that is the catalyst you need for change. A simple shift in view and perspective is all that is needed. Believe you can and you will. It is as simple as that.

What happens is we start to build evidence around our beliefs that help support our hypothesis. We look for examples around us that prove our point. For example, if all the friends and couples around us have failed in their relationships but are super successful in business then we correlate the two.

We start to normalise this in our minds and almost expect it; we totally disregard the other 50% of the population that does have both.

Now, granted, there are few outstanding examples of the perfect balance (maybe the pursuit of the ideal, the pinnacle of balance is a fruitless task, frankly!) but isn't the 'few outstanding examples' analogy true for outstanding businesses too? Yet we still choose to believe that business success is possible only by focusing on those few examples.

The second point to highlight is that you need to notice who you are measuring and comparing your success or standards by. Is what is happening what you really want and desire?

And if you are looking for examples then it is often said that you need to get 'proximity to power'. - Tony Robbins says that, and I have worked with him 1-2-1 so I can't disagree, but I would say that I prefer the idea of 'proximity to what you desire'.

Focus on what you want, not what you don't want.

This brings us on to the actionable steps to have a wife who desires you and will happily come to you when you call for her rather than do her work! The kind of relationship you want to come home to and not sit in the car on the driveway for thirty minutes, bracing yourself to come into a war zone, or not coming home to an empty apartment wishing there was someone you love waiting for you.

Here's the magic: you are not going to like it, but remember you are the elite 1%, prepared to do what it takes to get the outstanding life, wife and work. Right?

Here it is:

Believe you can have it all at an outstanding level.

Focus on what you want, not what you don't want.

Put the effort and time into learning and understanding the business of relationships.

Now, I know you are thinking, 'This is not rocket science, is it?' and you would be right. It is not. But the real question you need to be asking is, *'Am I implementing this in my life?'*

Where else have you implemented this unwavering focus on success in your life?

Work? Business? Kids?

Exactly.

How successful are they?

Creating seemingly effortless results? Exactly.

The same principles apply to relationships. The only problem is that you haven't applied the unwavering success focus in love and that, my beautiful dear friends, is the reason you haven't achieved a work, life, wife balance.

I know that some of you are really going to be triggered now. In some cases, massively. I'm sensing annoyance, frustration and possibly a feeling that reading this was a waste of your time. But I would love to ask you, how often do you dismiss as a waste of time information that triggers you? Is it possible that it is that very same information that you need to pay close attention to?

I am known for being the velvet glove with an iron fist. I look soft and elegant on the outside, but my delivery can have a hard iron punch to it. This is because it's the hard truths and questions in life that make the significant changes the fastest.

This book aims to provide you with the roadmap to you not only identifying but resolving those very triggers. You may be thinking that you have worked on these before with millions of counsellors/therapists. How is this going to be any different? It's because YOU are going to be in the driving seat. I am not going to spoon feed you because I trust you are a grown-arsed man! It's time to own it and be treated like one. I honour and trust you, and I respect men massively, being a converted man-hater to man-adorer. It's time to divorce the struggle, not the wife.

66

'SEE IT AS IT IS, NOT WORSE THAN IT IS.'

Tony Robbins

2

WHAT IS THE CURRENT POSITION?

I n this chapter we are going to understand your current position, and audit if you like. We only know where our starting point is when we understand how the land lies. We have to know where the roadmap starts

This chapter is going to be more fun and revealing than you think so it will be worth it.

Let's start with the obvious: you have everything you could possibly want and more. You have the houses, the cars, even the private jets and boats, and yet you feel like there is something missing. A sense of lack or loss or both, which at times drives you to distraction because on paper you 'should' be happy. You should feel in control, yet there is something inside you that is constantly chasing the next thing or the next woman. It's like there is a sense of dissatisfaction. It's like a duality that lives inside you, because you are well respected in your field and have people ask your advice daily, and you provide real mentorship for up-and-coming younger men. Interestingly enough, you get a real kick out of helping them for 'free'!

It's probably one of the one things, after your business success, that gives you the biggest natural high. Especially because you know these young men want and aspire to have what you have. There is a buzz about that yet also a sadness that, 'If only they knew it is not all it is cracked up to be,' or, 'In fact, it is pretty lonely at the top.' The worst thing of all is that you were once like those young men, wishing, dreaming, wanting, knowing you would 'have it all' one day and then you would be happy.

And there is the truth of it. None of it makes you happy. None of it makes you feel satisfied or successful. Just empty and lonely, because the one you thought was the love of your life causes nothing but heartache or you have entered this cycle of rotating through the same kind of women and a cycle of falling in 'love/lust'. It's amazing for a few years and then she starts to complain, you get tired and you move on. Sound familiar?

I told you I was going to be honest. I will give you nothing but the truth because I trust you can handle it and you deserve it. Most women struggle to believe that you can handle the truth. This might be hard to believe, but we often lie or hide things to protect you so you won't be upset with us. I add this as a side note to help you understand why sometimes women will appear to lie. In our heads we are protecting you from the truth so you don't react or shout.

I was one of those women before I started realising that men can take the truth and actually prefer it to the 'safety BS' I was feeding my hubby and the men in my life. If you want her to be honest, you have to acknowledge that it takes courage for her to speak directly and that rather than shouting or reacting you could pause and breathe and allow yourself the moment to 'feel' beyond the words.

Let's get on to helping you find the start of your roadmap.

I am going to take you through the process I use with my clients. Let me tell you what happened with 'Bob'. I have changed all names for the sake of privacy, of course.

Bob came to me out of the blue. I was in Spain attempting to write this book. I had been there for four months with very little progress. My Messenger on my phone rang from someone I didn't know. I think it is very strange, but my instinct told me to answer. I did and it was Bob's girlfriend, Tiffany, asking if I would see them for couples' coaching. I explained there was an application process and booked them into a Zoom interview. It became apparent straight away from that interview that Bob was lost and basically doing what he was told to keep Tiffany happy, but the truth he was weary. He had been walking that old worn-out path so many times. He sounded exhausted and in such despair.

He had an ex-wife who had 'poisoned' the children against him and now this woman was causing all kinds of problems and dragging him to a counsellor because he needed fixing! In meeting with me, he was ticking what he thought was a very expensive box. Let me paint the picture to help you put it into perspective. They had been together six years 'on and off'. She was in her forties, very attractive, and he was in his sixties and had made his millions from nothing. He came from a working-class family and had always been told by his father he was stupid and wouldn't amount to anything. And so he spent his life proving him wrong and boy, did he. He made it a multi-million-pound national business.

Along the way married the woman he thought was right, had two children, a boy and a girl. Gave them everything: the cars, holidays to Disneyland and all the trimmings. He had homes in London, Portugal and often spent Christmas in Dubai. On paper it looked like he had it all.

He was miserable because all he wanted was to be appreciated and acknowledged and all she wanted was more. It ended in a messy divorce and the mother of his children turning the children against him. She still chose not to work and was happy to have the handouts from him. He moved on to a newer model, who showered him with praise at the beginning. She came with a daughter. He took them both in and set her up in a little business and supported her jewelry passion. He paid for her daughter's private education and showered her with a fleet of cars, diamonds and even built her a brand-new mansion. The week they were due to move into the mansion, I got the call.

She said, 'Dimple, can you help? He needs fixing; he is so selfish and does nothing for me. I asked for this one thing in the mansion and he said no. He asked me to go to my mother's for a night because he needed a break and left me with nothing.'

Later I learned that she had the Range Rover and was still going visiting her horses (that he had given her). He had reached his limit and rather than fight, asked for a night off. The reason she was ringing me was because he wouldn't marry her and she wanted the commitment.

Are you getting a feel of what this looks like? I want to make it clear at this point that I am not siding with anyone. There is no right or wrong person. I believe we all have a path we decide to take and we are all responsible for our own actions. He allowed this to occur. She was coded from her upbringing to feel entitled. Those are the facts. We continue...

Of course, she believed she was the perfect girlfriend and couldn't understand why he didn't want to marry her. She would give back rubs and otherwise spend most of her time at work or with friends or with the horses. He was retired and was looking for a companion, lover and someone who appreciated him. From the outside it would look like he really ought to have married her. What otherwise was the point of the relationship? Where was it going? And that was the question they had both come to me with. They were both willing to try and give it a go. At least, she was willing as long as it was on her terms.

This may seem like I am on his side, but the truth is that I am telling the story of what I have experienced over and over again with more men than Bob. This is a pattern that men like Bob find themselves with very commonly. They move from one relationship to the next with very little awareness of their role in what and who they are attracting. It's like going into a car showroom thinking a new Ferrari will fix the problem of the broken Ferrari in the garage at home. All it does is massage the ego for a short while. Until that new Ferrari starts playing up. And then of course a Ferrari stops being their solution and they move to Lamborghinis and so the story continues. Did my point land? It's not the car or the girl that is the solution to the problem.

This couple, needless to say, didn't make it through the first two sessions. She couldn't take the truth and he had a very clear awakening and continued the coaching to heal the underlying problems/wounds and then attract the woman of his dreams.

She wasn't ready to do the work and moved to the next wealthy man who she believed would make her happy. No judgement, just everyone has their own unique path.

The lessons of this story are:

1. What we think we want isn't what we actually need.
2. The grass is not always greener.
3. We have to discover the real problem and fix that, not the one that is on the surface. Dig deeper or repeat history.
4. Learn the lesson otherwise you know you are going to be given the same lesson to learn again but bigger!

Understanding these three points revolutionises relationships for men. When we can truly see the situation from all perspectives, we can then have a deeper understanding of the problem and therefore a solution that is a win for all. This comes as a result of focusing on the truth, not your blind spots (which we all have, including me) or our ego/dick driven truth. Sorry, not sorry: it had to be said. I believe there are four centres a man makes a decision from:

1. Ego
2. Heart
3. Gut
4. Dick

The centre that is running the show in relationships will determine the success of the relationship. I am sure you can guess, if you want a fulfilling life, which one not to allow to run the show. If you want to be a playboy in your fifties and sixties then you would use a very different centre. There is no wrong or right, you just have to know what your end point is and then reverse engineer your roadmap. There is no ego here, just insight into understanding who is running the show and are they the right MD for the job?

Think about your life and areas of your life as if they are individual businesses within your empire. Your relationship is one business, work is another, family another and so on. Each corporation has a board of directors. The one for your relationship has MD Ego, MD Heart, MD Gut and MD Dick. All have very important roles to play in the corporation of relationship. Now if one MD is more outspoken than the others, that will determine the direct and outcome of the success of the business, right? So the key to a successful business is knowing when and how you lead and support each MD. That requires a very skilled CEO.

He develops the skills of perfect timing, when to say yes or no, who to allow to lead and for how long. They can see the bigger picture but only as a result of making many mistakes along the way. This book is all about gifting you the skills and experience, as much as I can within a book, of my years as a CEO of many men's, couples' and women's business of relationship and life legacy planning. This is helping you find YOUR PURPOSE. Helping you answer the question of why you were put on this planet. This brings me nicely to this question.

I ask tough questions in this book and this is one of those questions:

'What do you want? Playboy life or life partner? Which makes you happy? Be truthful. Does your current 'success' make you happy?

I want you to sit with these questions, answer them honestly, without judging yourself. There is no right or wrong, just clarity in truth. This will help you set the red pin on your roadmap.

We will dig deeper into that at another point of the book: I just wanted to plant the seed. For now I want us to focus on where you are at this stage and therefore why you struggle to lead in your relationships.

66

"DEEP IN HIS HEART, EVERY
MAN LONGS FOR A BATTLE
TO FIGHT, AN ADVENTURE
TO LIVE, AND A BEAUTY TO
RESCUE."

John Eldredge

3

WHY DON'T CEOS LEAD IN THEIR RELATIONSHIPS?

I n this chapter we are going to dive deeper into why successful men/CEOs become mice when they turn the key of the front door of their mansion, fearing their women, and I will introduce you to my 3 S's framework of what happens when you stop leading in a relationship. Before I do that though, I want to explain why it is so important for the man to lead in a romantic relationship. I know a lot of women are screaming at me saying, 'We don't live in Victorian times, you know! Women don't need a man.' Truthfully, it is those same women that are lonely and hurting inside and here is why.

Our brains have not developed much in this area since we were cavemen and women. At its simplest form, men are programmed to provide and protect and women are programmed to nurture and seduce. Men give and women receive. I know what you are thinking, where are these women? because all the ones I have been with tell me they give all the time and I take! And this has been the problem - Women have lost the art of receiving resulting in men being too fearful to give. Now this is its crudest form but think about it for a moment. How good does it feel for you when you give your wife a beautiful gift of your time or something physical and she truly appreciates it with her smile or words? Nothing major, just a 'thank you' and a genuine smile! It's priceless. Why is that? That is because somewhere inside you, you are designed to protect and provide. If a woman was in danger in the street, most men would instantly go to her rescue. Why? Another example, crude again but powerful is intercoarse. I mean who gives and who receives? The man goes into the women and she receives his sacred DNA.

And I don't care how many independent, financially successful women there are. I haven't met one who doesn't desire her man to take charge and control. Now, let's be clear, it is not about who has the biggest bank balance but how he makes her feel safe and protected. This could look like making the dinner reservations, making the **decisions,** taking the lead. I know many of you have made decisions in the past and taken control and it has been thrown back in your face and so you never do it again for fear of rejection. I understand this is very painful. What if you could see her push back as a test of your manhold? Because even though she may not be aware of it, women are innately designed to test our men, we can't help it. Now that doesn't mean it is right and a conscious woman would present it much more compassionately than a less mature woman. Believe me this is a whole masterclass in itself. My testing at the beginning of our marriage was brutal compared to now and yes it still happens, because we are testing to know how strong you are not questioning your decision or manhood.

'Welcome the women''s test like you would the challenge of the last climb to the peak of Everest. It's a badge of honour not shame.'

It is very important, especially as women are rising in their presence in the workforce as equals (and so they should), that the purpose of a modern-day relationship is not for the man to provide financial support and the woman to stay at home and take care of the home and children, but that it is based on love. It's an exciting time of evolution of modern-day relationships. However, many couples are navigating blindly this duality of wanting the equal relationship but still feeling the innate pull to go back to traditional roles in intimate relationships, hence the constant battle resulting in multiple relationship failures. How this may present itself is described next and results in my 3 S's framework.

It is highly likely you have failed a few times in your relationships. Maybe you've even been divorced once or twice and you are finding yourself asking, "How is it that I can nail building a successful business with all the complexity of relationships that this requires – but I can't do it in love?"

The answer to this question is very simple and I will explain *exactly* why.

Let's take a look at how you have got to this point in your life. Why? Because life leaves clues!

I am guessing, even if you are not divorced, you have not had the easiest journey when it comes to keeping the wife happy, right? You have tried everything. Provided her with all she could want and she just seems cold, angry, disconnected or all of the above.

It never started that way; in the beginning, before you had anything, she was light, bright and glowed. The sex was incredible and you were enough for her.

As the years went on and you became more successful, possibly at the same time as the children came along, and things changed. She became distant; you became less of her focus. She was distracted or tired. She was often criticising you or telling you where you were going wrong. She made you feel as though you couldn't win and nothing you were doing was good enough. And at the same time you noticed a hardness in her face. She lost her glow.

Life at home has become effortful and, instead of it being a place of sanctuary and peace, the house has become a place of conflict. This presents in more ways than one. Silence or screaming, you never quite know which one you are going to be greeted with as you turn the key.

In fact, it has become so exhausting that you prefer to be at work and find yourself delaying coming home. Spending more and more time at work and who can blame you? Why would you want to go home to be made to feel small when at work you are a king?

Besides, there are no 'French' benefits any more either! There is no point; you can't win either way.

If any (or all) of the above resonates, here are the 3 S's of what will occur next:

Settle - You stay and become a silent roommate and lose who you are. I know this is happening when I hear my executive clients say, 'I have lost my manhood' or 'I have lost who I am.' Their beliefs about marriage, their upbringing or simply their internal rules on 'failing' keep them in a miserable existence and they just get their wins at work. You will have experienced this couple. They have usually been married for at least a decade. The man looks weary and tired, like he is defeated. Life has worn him down. He rarely voices his opinion and is very loyal. His wife talks to him like a child and she looks old and weathered and exhausted with making all the decisions. She wears the trousers in the relationship. You will often see her walking ahead of him. He walks slowly, with his shoulders stooped and rounded and rarely lifts his head. He is just existing. Waiting to be happy or die.

Separate - You leave and blame the wife for changing you, never learning how to solve this problem and you go on repeating this same pattern over and over again. You don't realise that the common denominator is YOU. I recognise this in my clients who talk of all their failed relationships being the fault of the women. She was vindictive and manipulative. He says, 'It started by being amazing and then she turned on me.' He is addicted to the honeymoon stage of every relationship and when it reaches the love and growth stage, what I call autumn /fall, he bails because it is too much hard work or effort. This man continues to go from one relationship to the next and never really grows in the area of relationships. He gets more and more disillusioned with women and ends his life either single or unhappy in love as he formulates the belief that women are manipulators. He never really understands or takes radical responsibility for his part in his relationship journey.

Stray - You have an affair because your need for physical and emotional connection becomes too overwhelming for you to ignore. The animal instinct or Dick MD takes over. Let's make it clear there is no judgement here, just facts. The male brain is designed from caveman times to procreate, hence the reason why in general men think about sex more than women. It is no coincidence that Dick is one of the centres of control for a man. I am not condoning adultery but simply explaining why this category exists. If a man feels trapped, lost or undervalued some men will transition from settling to reaching their breaking point, at which they can no longer manage their emotional and sexual needs not being met in their relationship and will seek comfort and being wanted elsewhere. This is often driven by the ego and dick centres and is never a happy ending because the pattern just continues.

Does this framework sound familiar to you?

You may have even experienced this several times already; either with the same woman or different women. You are probably seeing this with such clarity for the first time and recognising patterns in your life where you have moved from one or more of the categories.

The most profound realisation for men is that there is another S and that they don't need to keep going round and round the loop. The final S is the deal breaker, the game changer. The one that breaks the cycle and provides true happiness and freedom. All those 3 S's just put a plaster on the wound, they don't actually heal it. Now we have established what the problem is and the outcomes that most CEOs 'choose'... let's talk about the fourth S.

Solve - This is the man who decided to learn and understand the best relationship. He gets an education and actually heals the wound rather than putting a plaster on it.

So what is the solution? How do you stop yourself from repeating history? First, know it is only the top 1% who are prepared to go here. If you have read this far then I want to congratulate you as you are in that top 1% by just reading this.

Here is the solution:

Understand that she didn't change you; you decided to change to make her happy. You can't make her happy - only she can. Your job is to be you and grow in your manhood. Be more of you and she will love you even more. You 'be' more for you first, then for her and finally for the relationship.

The solution is so simple, yet the effort is required in the execution.

The next question is, why do CEOs, who are kings at work, turn into mice as soon as they walk in the door? This is such a fascinating thing. Having worked with many high-level CEOs (and being married to one) there is a trend that I have noticed.

CEOs are unique beasts in their own way but very often they have shared characteristics:

Drive and tenacity beyond the vast majority of people.

Willingness to dedicate the extraordinary energy, effort and time it takes to become a CEO.

Extremely high standards and rules for their perfect life.

Calculated risk-takers.

Huge fear/frustration of failing.

These characteristics are incredible for success at work but can create problems in relationships if you are not conscious of them and don't have strategies of how to 'switch' from being CEO to a husband or partner.

Here is what I mean...

There have been times in my marriage, especially at the beginning, when my man would talk to me like one of his employees or clients - this showed up via:

His tone

Interrupting me

Finishing my sentences before me

Taking charge without asking my opinion

Overruling or undermining my decisions

Do any of these sound familiar? See, you are not alone.

The behaviours above will make your woman/wife want to:

Control you

Criticise you

Close you off

Keep sex from you

Let's discuss for a minute what this might look like. She will say she is fine, in that tone by which you clearly know she is not and yet you won't have a clue about what you have done wrong. She will hold a grudge and give you the silent treatment and withhold sex for weeks and you won't have a clue as to why. Things that didn't bother her before suddenly start to bother her, like the way you breathe, or that you didn't take the trash out immediately, or the way you made her coffee.

Instead of praise you will find her criticising or finding fault with your every move. These are all symptoms of a woman not heard and the solution is NOT to stay away and feel attacked. The reason she does all this is because when she doesn't feel in control and safe she will protect herself, because she doesn't feel you will provide protection. You become a threat and as you are physically stronger, the only way we instinctively know how to protect ourselves is to take back control by attacking your Achilles' heel - your heart and dick centres.

All women instinctively know how to do this and are not afraid to use it. It's our weapon and we watch our mothers, sisters, aunties and grandmothers use it to control and manipulate men and so we grow up thinking this is the only way to protect ourselves. It's awful but true. Women are so unconscious to this and the impact it has on men, including myself until I did the work on me. Most women are walking around unconscious and I am sure my next book will be for them. But in the meantime, how can you fix this problem and improve your relationship without losing you and make her happy at the same time? In other words, how do you fix it?

One simple word... Listen.

Before I go into how you do this, because I can hear all the men saying, 'But I do listen, I hear every word,' I want to explain why this is so important and the impact on her when you get this right and when you don't. In other words, the results, the outcome.

Remember when I was explaining why sex is more important to the male brain than to women because it dates back to primitive times when men's primary function was to procreate. Now let's consider why listening is just as important to a woman as searching for sex is for you. When you search for the right mate, the right look and compatibility are the precursors for procreating for you. Listening is the precursor for a woman, not for sex but for something that is equally important to her. Yes, you heard me, there is something that has just the same degree of importance to women and that is SAFETY.

She thinks about safety probably the same number of times you think about sex in a day. Let's go back to the primitive brain to work out why. While you went out to hunt, the women were left unprotected and so would sit in circles protecting each other through listening, talking and watching each other. This gave them a sense of safety, especially sat all together, hence safety in numbers. It is the reason women go to the restroom in groups and why this wouldn't even occur to men. Is it becoming clearer now? Can you *hear* why listening to her is so important and why when she doesn't feel you are listening to her, she feels unsafe and then jumps into protector mode, also known as the bitch from hell or the crazy lady for no logical reason.

Now I hear you and I know you listen and can recite everything she has said word for word, but there is a real strategy and formula by which she needs to feel heard. If this formula is not followed, then it doesn't matter how much you hear her; it will be a waste of your energy. I am about to introduce you to a concept that I realised while studying men's and women's communication styles, needs and desires. I like to take big concepts and simplify them, that is how my brain works. The concept I want to explain will help you understand where you are going wrong and how to fix it. It will result in her feeling heard and you being the source of her safety and guess what happens when she feels safe? She doesn't have to protect herself. The crazy lady doesn't appear. That's right, no criticising, bitching, saying 'I'm fine' when you know she isn't, and more sex for you. I know you can't believe it is this simple.

It is the communication currency. Men and women communicate with a different currency. Imagine trying to buy groceries in NYC with rupees? It's not possible to purchase a damn thing. Does it mean the rupee is worthless? No. Does it mean the groceries aren't worth their cost? No. It just means the wrong currency in the wrong place. Mismatch, that is all.

There are two different currencies of exchange. This means that men operate in **'facts'** and women operate in **'feelings'**.

I hear the men say, '*Well, that doesn't make any sense because how are 'feelings' a thing?*' They aren't measurable or objective. Whereas **'facts'…** you can hold and grab facts. They are tangible. They are 'real'.

Let me demonstrate.

Male perspective: So the fact is, '*I heard every word!*'

Female perspective: The feeling is, '*Yes, you did, but I didn't feel that you heard me.*'

She knows you heard every word - fact! She knows you can repeat every word she said. She understands that you can listen and there is nothing wrong with your ears. All these facts, believe it or not, she is fully aware of, though it may not seem like it in the moment.

You might still ask what the problem is, because now this makes no logical sense. None whatsoever!

Well, now you understand that she deals in 'feelings' and you deal in 'facts'. I'd like you to imagine that someone says that you are not financially successful even though your success is a fact based on your bank account. Further imagine that they continue to say it, even though the fact is you are financially successful. They are questioning your currency, right? The facts.

Well, this is in fact (excuse the pun) what you are doing when you tell her she is wrong because you heard everything and yes, you were listening! Now breathe. I am coming to the point.

Her currency is feelings. She is not basing her comment on facts but on how you left her feeling! When you were listening did you put your mind in neutral to listen and learn or did you listen until she got to the point so that you could speak?

Be honest. There is no judgement, we just want to establish facts because the next thing that I am going to reveal to you is the game changer. This will take your conversations from helpless to hero.

There is an art to making a woman feel heard and it is much simpler than you think BUT it requires high focus and intentionality. Very few men achieve this well but when they do, oh, my God! It is magic!

Here it is:

Focused listening. This is the art of listening to your woman so she feels heard.

1. Set the intention that you want to learn and get curious about her.
2. Put your brain into neutral, not resting or waiting to talk while she assesses for problem mode.
3. Stop everything else you are doing (trust me, this will save you time in the long run).
4. Clear the decks for any interruptions.

5. Look at her - in the eye.
6. The whole time she is talking from your heart repeat you are safe, I protect you, I love you - feel it not speak it and send her that feeling to her heart.
7. Let her talk.
8. Do not scan for problems. The problem is not at the end. The problem is you scanning for the problem and not listening with the intention to understand her.
9. The outcome of the conversation is to only make her '**feel**' heard by doing all these steps.
10. When she is complete, she will sigh. That is when you know she is done.

This may seem very effortful but it is much less effort than having the same BS arguments over not being heard.

Let me review why her feeling '**heard**' is so vital. When she '**feels**' heard she feels seen and when she feels seen she feels safe. If you are the person hearing and seeing her then you are the source of her safety. Remember the tribe sitting in a circle, watching and hearing each other to keep each other SAFE from the saber tooth tiger . Looking and listening = safety.

That is how you get to be her hero because safety is her number one priority. A woman will do anything it takes to feel safe - even pushing away her man if she doesn't feel safe with him. In other words, she feels not heard! The clues are in the behaviour, not the words she speaks.

To really bring this home, let me explain again how significant safety is for her. It has the same weighting sex has for you. What would you do for more sex, connection and intimacy?

To summarise, gentlemen, if you:

1. Listen to learn rather than getting your point across
2. Focus on her
3. Give her eye contact

Then this is the game changer in moving from facts to her feelings being heard. When you start communicating in her currency you'd better be ready for the happy, sexy, beautiful woman you desire. She won't be able to keep her hands off you.

Make way, boys, the MAN has just stepped into the room!

I know it is hard to believe it could be that 'simple', but when was the last time you really listened without interrupting her? Do you try to get your point of view across or assume you know where she is going in the conversation and rush her to the end?

If you can master the art of listening without wanting to 'fix the problem' you will witness a massive change in her. Because of the change in YOU.

Think about the beginning of the relationship; how often did you listen? Were you curious to get to know her? Of course you were!

I am not a mind reader, but I know what you are thinking... 'All the above sounds fine, Dimple, but she never stops talking!'

Well, the truth is, if you are not *really* listening, just waiting to talk instead of wanting to learn her point of view, then she will feel it. And here is what will happen - she will keep talking! Why? Because she thinks she hasn't explained herself well enough and needs to either a) repeat it, or b) explain in a different way until you understand.

You not learning to listen actually delays the whole process. So save yourself time, effort and your marriage. Listen to learn and learn to listen. That is how a true King leads at home.

I deliberately use the language of 'king' because it is one of the stages of a man. I first learnt of the development of stages of a man at a Tony Robbins relationship seminar in Maui. The very same event took my then twenty-year marriage from the brink of divorce back to teenaged lovers and beyond. We have just celebrated our 26th wedding anniversary. If I had known this same strategy when we were in the infancy of our relationship, it would have saved us so much heartache.

In the next chapter I am going to describe the different stages and how they impact how you navigate your life. The decisions you make, the sacrifice you have made and the impact on your intimate relationships.

**'MEN ARE A GIFT FROM
GOD TO WOMEN.'**

Alison Armstrong

4

THE LIFE STAGES OF A MAN

It is with great sadness this week (at time of writing) that we hear of another power couple Bill and Melinda Gates divorcing after 27 years of marriage. One could say, *having been through the painstaking growth season of their marriage,* to come to the time when they should be reaping the fruits of their labour, why would they quit now? After almost three decades together surely they know each other well enough to navigate the sometimes choppy waters of a relationship? Well, actually, the real reason for this despondent outcome has a lot to do with Bill being *in the tunnel* and neither of them knowing how to navigate it.

You are probably wondering what *the tunnel* is? If you are a highly successful executive male in your forties or fifties, it is likely that you are experiencing the tunnel now and have no idea.

The tunnel was first described by relationship guru Alison Armstrong and when I first heard of it at a Tony Robbins Platinum partners event **it blew my mind**, because it was the answer to *so many questions*. So many reasons why my man behaved the way he did in each decade of our lives together.

The tunnel is actually part of the life cycle of most men and, given that the phenomenon is so prevalent, it makes sense to try and spread awareness around this so that **both** men and women can understand.

I believe that every man and wife should understand the cycle and where they are in relation to it. Why? Because it provides people with an interpretation as to why they focus on what they do in each phase of their life... (Just to note: there is also a life cycle of a woman too, but we are not covering that in this book. Let's focus on one thing at a time.)

Recognising the tunnel helps your wife understand that you aren't ignoring her. If I had understood this cycle at the beginning of my marriage it would have stopped me from believing that my man was having an affair!

That's right, the relationship expert - *with over two decades of experience* - felt she was second fiddle to another woman. But it turned out not to be a **'who'** that had his attention and focus but a **'what'**. What I was *actually* insanely jealous of was 'The Business'. His work. The thing for which he stayed away from our home, our children and from me for 12-16 hours a day.

In our own relationship, the tunnel concept gave my man the power to understand his drivers and why his need to provide during certain phases in his life, was *unstoppable* and, at times - from my perspective - unbearable. This realisation enabled answers to why he came home day after day at 11pm and then had the drive to get up again the next day and leave for 'The Business' at 6am.

Understanding that the life cycle *changes* and *pivots* and *fluctuates* and *modifies* also offers an explanation as to why he no longer desires that level of 'hustle' now and why his priorities are different.

Have I expressed *enough* the importance of knowing where you are, where you have been and where you are heading in your life and relationship?

Good, because understanding the tunnel can be essential to relationships - in some cases **saving them entirely.**

It is so interesting because when I explained this to one of my highly successful friends (and when I say successful, I mean he has sold seven companies successfully for nine figures each, that kind of guy) his mind was blown. He couldn't believe that he was also in the tunnel - he was on the journey himself!

He actually started to play a game with his newfound perceptive knowledge. He could look at another successful executive and name exactly where this man was in his own life. He started to enjoy his new sage-like wisdom so much that he'd start assessing the level of 'tunnelitus' when he was having coffee, in the shops - spotting tunnel-stages while just out and about!

So, having *teased* the fact that the tunnel is the answer to so many questions - shall I now take you on a journey through it... Ok, great, we are you ready, here we go!

Phase One: The Pauper

Typically below the age of 18. This guy is just curious about the world, takes massive risks and is completely unaware of the consequences. The reason young boys leap off high walls or furniture or, when they hit the teenage years, they play games like 'chicken' (you know, the one where you run across the highway aiming to avoid the cars) is because they have **nothing to lose**. They are poor. Zero consequences.

Phase Two: The Knight

Aged 18 to 30 years old. Typically he is in exploration mode in all areas of life; work, play, love, growth. A male entrepreneur in this phase would be chasing every deal that comes to them, and usually every girl. They are learning the craft of work and women. If they are in relationships they are usually restless to explore and do this in their work. If they are single they would be 'playing the field'.

I remember this phase well with my husband. He was clubbing every night, holding down three jobs as well as doing his degree and was *always on the hunt for the next deal*. His work ranged from selling mangos on the market to designer suits in high-end shops. He was basically *having a go at everything.* There is usually energy, speed and a sense of rushing - this is normally coupled with zero concern at not knowing it all.

This phase is very difficult for a wife or partner to live with if she isn't aware that it is a phase! From my own experience, I didn't understand it and so, *from the outside looking in,* I thought he was wasting time and would continually ask myself (and occasionally him) why couldn't he just get a proper job? Why did he need to go sell mangos for pennies? I just didn't get it. The *'it'* was this urge for him to grow through exploring everything. It is and was a vital part of his development and success now.

Phase Three: The Prince

Aged between 30-45. Alternatively known as 'the settling down phase'. This is when his brain can switch suddenly, like a light bulb, overnight; he realises what his gift is, what his genius is, where he excels through all the trial and error of the knighthood. He has clarity in his goals at work and home. It is usually the time when children come on the scene and this is a huge motivator to 'provide'. It is a period of focused and 'directed' expansion. It was the time when my husband realised he was gifted in the world of finance, doubled down his attention and made this area his main focus - which translated into it becoming his biggest area of fiscal benefit.

Thank God he gave up selling the *bloody* mangos on a Sunday at an ungodly hour for pennies. Although I say that in jest (*mostly!*) it is really important for a wife to (try!) not tell him what is the 'obvious' thing he needs to do during phase two. The reality is that he will come into phase three much quicker if there isn't too much pressure from the partner in that regard; he has to have the realisation himself that the mangos aren't going to make millions!

However, what he learnt from all the jobs through the initial phases was how to finance and structure every industry going. It was his 'apprenticeship' in readiness of finding his true passion, which is structuring deals and finance for large organisations. What I considered to be time wasting was the foundation to understanding the nuances of each industry. Nothing is wasted time. Boy, I wished I had known this then. It would have saved so much time and heartache... for both of us.

The third phase is usually the building phase in which he is honing his craft and growing his empire. It requires a lot of focus, time and energy. Usually, it is slap bang at the same time the wife needs exactly that too, because during the midst of the growth phase is usually when the pitter patter of tiny feet kicks in. This is the phase when the 3 S's that I talked about in my previous chapter occur. It is a very challenging time for a lot of couples; 50% survive but only a very small percentage of that 50% actually thrive. This was around the time I decided to become the crazy lady. I am going to reveal a story that wasn't one of my finest moments but at the time I felt so justified. The point of this story is to help you understand that her motives are not to attack you but are actually quite the opposite. Here we go, I am about to get real and raw for the greater good of all...

We were year five into our marriage and looking back he was definitely in prince mode, although I didn't know it at the time. All I saw was a man who cared more about selling mangos on a Sunday morning at some godly hour than he did about spending time with the daughter he wanted. I know, it's so harsh, but honestly that is exactly how I felt. I didn't want children, and even if I did, I didn't expect to put my life on hold full time. I thought it would be a joint effort, but no, I was *expected* to do it all, work full time, do nursery runs at both ends of the day, be the main bread winner, cook, clean, and be provider of sex with zero return on investment.

Guys, you are getting the insides of your wife's brain here and if you don't believe me, ask her. If she is your ex, still ask her.

One Sunday morning he said he would be back at 2pm and we can have some family time together. I thought, *Yeah, right - he has never been back before 4!*

I had had four weeks 24/7 managing everything and I was done! It didn't even enter my mind that he had also done 24/7 for four weeks straight with no family time. I assumed he had chosen that and he was having fun with 'the mistress' (The

Business), while I was doing a thankless task raising our family. You know the *children he wanted*.

When I look back now it saddens my heart to think I thought so little of him and didn't see the efforts he was putting in for us to have a better life and didn't value the role that I was playing in raising our incredible family. Hindsight is a wonderful thing. –

I said to him as he left that if he wasn't back by 2pm we were finished. I was done and I was throwing him out! I had reached a point of no return. A woman needs three things from her relationship, from you. Only you can provide these for her. With these three things she will feel on top of the world and you will be her reason why. You will be her hero because when you provide these consistently and wholeheartedly you will 'own' your woman. They are so simple but very few men execute them correctly. It was these three things that I was so deprived of and this turned me into the crazy lady. Once these things are implemented they can reverse all the damage done from the past and she will be putty in your hands. But before I reveal what these are I need to finish the story.

He agreed to come home at 2pm so off he went at 6am. I got on with my morning fun with Maya, our two-year-old daughter. I had already planned what I was going to do. I took a photo of the door lock and I strapped Maya into her car seat and drove twenty minutes to the hardware store. I hunted down the man who could tell me exactly what I needed to know to execute my plan and what equipment I would need to do it. Now

I am a 5' 2" Indian lady with no idea about how to use a drill, never mind what I was about to execute. I made my purchase and hoped Maya would stay asleep long enough after lunch for me to complete the task in hand. I put her to bed and I was possessed: game plan on. If he didn't honour his word I certainly would. It took me twenty mins to find the toolbox in the garage (that was not my domain of the house), then I had to find the right tool. The man at the hardware store said I needed to measure and then file down to length. Ok so I was thinking a nail file was what I would use to file so maybe there was a tool that looked like a nail file. I found one, but the thing I had to file was a solid metal bar about 50mm thick.

I am a Taurean. Some would say stubborn; I call it determined. I filed for ninety mins solid. My fingers blistered. I knew *he* would know a quicker way, but I was on my own now I would learn. I did it bang on 2pm. Mission complete. The locks were changed. I felt so proud of myself. Maya had stayed asleep the whole time.

I was covered in blisters and he was nowhere to be seen. I knew it. I was right. I cared more about being right than losing the love of my life. Then I waited and waited and waited at the bay window of our first home together. It was a beautiful detached home that we had lovingly painted together. We had very little furniture but we were so proud to be in it.

Bang on 4pm his car pulled up in front of the house. There was only room for one car on the drive and he always let me have that spot. Looking back, he looked so tired and weary and I didn't even notice, because I was full of anger and resentment. Remember, I was deprived of the three vitals a woman needs from her man.

I watched from the window as he attempted to use his key to let himself in. He tried a few times and I watched him from the bay window with a stern face as if to say *I told you I would.* Guys, you know the face all women have. The 'don't mess with me face.' He begged and pleaded with me to let him in, then sat in his car for two hours. Eventually I broke and we made up.

The point of this story is to help both the men and the women understand that nobody is right or wrong, and if we can view from the lens of the other person then our perspective and outcome is based on love not being right.

What are the three things a woman needs, then? They are not a big house, fancy car and nice handbag. The three things are to *feel safe, seen and heard.*

To summarise the prince stage: business is growing and the family is growing which usually means responsibility is growing and pressure is growing - it's no wonder that households can sometimes become a tinderbox at this point!

It is so sad because if people knew that the drive and determination to *work so hard* was to provide and the *overwhelming, unstoppable urge* he has to give the family security is something he can't help, then maybe those fractious conversations at home would subside. I know for sure I would have given far more grace. I would have looked at his behaviour very differently and put different meaning on it, which would have therefore created different responses. Lets face it this is a question I ask a lot of the wives I work with, 'Would you want to live with you?' Ouch! Because the truth is I wouldn't want to live with that version of me back then.

Having said all the above, hang in there, fellas, because it gets even 'better' for you guys in phase 4 - so much empathy for you beautiful men now.

Phase Four: The Tunnel

I am actually shaking writing this phase. Having witnessed my man going through this phase and knowing the pain that he endured, you would not wish this on your worst enemy. Only through understanding was I able to support him out of it.

This phase is from age 45 and lasts decades.

Yes, you read it right, for decades. This is where a lot of men stay and die. This phase is commonly referred to as the infamous 'mid-life crisis'. It's a time in his life where he has made his 'millions' and he has everything material he needs. His life looks so good on paper, but he is not happy. This can appear in different ways:

1. He becomes distant or distracted, spending large amounts of time alone.
2. Or he becomes obsessed with toxic or destructive relationships because they look good from the outside.
3. He is worried about not fulfilling his purpose and dying unsuccessful, having not left a legacy for the planet.
4. He starts to act out of character.
5. He will often say he feels lost and alone.

It is important to note that this is a general rule for most 'healthy' men. If you have mental health conditions please refer to your doctor/clinician.

He feels something is missing; he is lacking something. He is lost. He is searching for his ultimate **'why?'** He usually, at this stage, starts doing crazy things like buying sports cars and wondering if his wife of twenty years is the right one? Is the grass greener? This is the phase in which he potentially commits the cardinal sin of the all too common extra-marital affair.

He travels or takes up strange hobbies. He seeks adventure and a mission-based legacy. For the first time in a long time, he has all the resources but is very confused regarding what life is all about.

I like to call this phase 'the darkness'. He can see the light at the end of the tunnel but doesn't know how to get there. He often feels like a failure or that he is unsuccessful. Usually this can - unfortunately - coincide with the wife going through menopause and her finding her voice and deciding that the years of neglect and loneliness have to come to a head.

It is a time in their lives when they have everything and they should be happy; they should be enjoying the fruits of their labour and instead he is disconnected and she has had enough. To her, he is uninterested, and she feels that after all these years she is still not enough, especially if he has an affair with a 'younger model'.

Before I understood this phase I remember feeling neglected for a long time, to the point where we were heading for a divorce. I was 42 and he was 48 and we sat and sighed one evening after what had become the normal cycle of a week of love and happiness, followed by three weeks of fighting, exhaustion, cold shoulder, silence and not touching or talking. I was the ice queen. It was like sleeping next to a plank of frozen wood.

The more we entered this cycle the more we became miserable and further away from what we really both wanted so desperately, which was respect, love and connection. The more we tried to get our points of view understood the less we understood each other. We reached this point one day when we both said we loved each other enough to let each other go because we felt there was no other option. It was time to plan THE DIVORCE.

It was a sad day. I felt my heart had been torn out of my body. He started planning the logistics. We agreed on a date - our 25th wedding anniversary as we had calculated our children would be 16 and 21, old enough to understand. We agreed on these three years to plan it like a business exit.

This was all while he was in the tunnel and I had no idea about this phase for a man. It is brutal and the impact for the woman and the relationship can be devastating. I truly believe this is the main reason you hear of couples divorcing after 25 years of being married, like Melinda and Bill Gates.

It was only through the courage of me taking a deep dive into this work were we able to heal ourselves and then our marriage - celebrating 26 years of marriage next month. The process can be reversed and evolved very fast - it took us eight weeks with my methods and healing that I use with my one to one executive clients. It often results in them saying, 'I wish I had met you twenty years ago, Dimple. I would still be happily married to the mother of my children, my biggest regret.'

There is only one way to get out of the tunnel, you can't avoid it or try to bypass it, you have to go through it to grow through it and very few couples make it.

Phase Five: The King

This is what is at the end of the tunnel: the light! During this phase, the man has his established kingdom and his people come to him for advice. He usually has a queen who has helped him out of the tunnel and they work in partnership to support the kingdom, that is, the family, business, etc. The energy behind a King is calmness, self-assurance and respect. The work is humanitarian and for the collective. Very few men ever reach this but all men strive for it.

I believe this phase is the phase most men aspire to but never reach. Many don't even believe it exists. This is why it is so important to speak and learn about it. Imagine a world where you feel so certain and sure about your decisions and you have the support of a woman who is fully aligned and stands in her power. She is willing to surrender to you and trust you at the same time as challenging you to grow. This provides you with both peace and freedom at once.

Sounds like the dream, right?

This comes with a level of deep understanding and commitment to personal growth first. The mistake most couples make is that they over give for years and years and years until the men become addicted to pleasing and the women become exhausted with wearing the trousers. They both believe they are givers and they build resentment towards each other and the relationship. The reason I describe this process here is to harness the magnitude of work that has to be achieved and maintained in order to grow and achieve King and Queen-hood. That is why the tunnel is decades. Having experienced the tunnel for two decades and only just fully understanding what it takes to support a man to kinghood, I realise the magnitude of work and effort required. So know that this information is not just textbook stuff but real life, done and doing the work experience. I don't write about anything I haven't experienced myself.

So the real question is how do you get to become a KING?

The first step is to become aware of which stage you are at now and honour it, with acceptance and awareness. Don't rush. It's a process. It is not about winning the race, it's about experiencing the journey; think hare and tortoise. All the experiences, all the obstacles and lessons learnt are needed to formulate the wisdom of a king. This means the decades, or apprenticeship, of the tunnel. It's only when you can really weather the darkness of the fiercest storm that you build that muscle of experience and wisdom of a king.

In summary, be aware of where you are, acknowledge it, don't rush and give gratitude to each step of the way. Many high achievers and all my clients when they realise they are in the tunnel the next question they ask is: How do I become a King and get out of the tunnel? Rushing this process rather than acknowledging and being grateful for it will only extend the tunnel and delay if not prevent you from becoming a king.

Slow down to speed up. Enjoy the ride, switch the word obstacle as opportunity to expand.

The second part is to stop ignoring your gut - your gut is there as your internal barometer. It will never let you down. Yet how many times do you ignore it for an easy life? Or to please her because you don't want to deal with the upset? Here's what happens when you become addicted to pleasing - in a nutshell, nobody grows. It's the coward's way out. It takes guts to stand up for what you believe to be true and it's why you have a gut instinct. Men have been gifted gut instinct for one reason and one reason only.

To PROTECT and PROVIDE for **ALL**.

That means that when a man makes a decision from his gut he is making it not just for him but his internal barometer has already calculated the risks versus the benefits for ALL!

That's right, the greater good of ALL.

Unfortunately, what has happened in society is that men have fewer and fewer role models of men who honour their gut instinct and follow through because of the rise in single parent families and a generation of men being raised in single mothers. This results in mothers being their significant role models. The problem with that is that women don't have the same gut instinct and while they are doing a job beyond what I could even begin to imagine, they just don't have the same hard wiring as men. Compounded by absent fathers and the resentment of that, it's no wonder men in today's society are confused. Do I open the door for her or not? Is it ok to say 'No' to a woman if I believe it is the wrong thing to do even if I know she will be upset for a short while? All these questions only a great male role figure can model.

Finally, the third piece of learning is to understand and source all your love and energy from within. That is, bring the whole of you to the relationship not 50/50. Most couples start a relationship or marriage feeling they need the other person to complete them. This is a co-dependent relationship. The problem with that is you set you and your partner up to fail. Why? Because they will never complete you. Only you can do that. If you can only feel love and happiness from them and they aren't there or they are having a bad day, then you feel lack and depleted. The worst thing about this is if you are the partner who is expected to keep them happy it is a huge responsibility. Can you see how most couples navigate life like this and wonder why they never feel fulfilled even though they have all the materialistic things in the world? They have the cars, houses and holidays but still feel lack.

The key is to be interdependent. That means you source love and happiness from yourself not from anyone else. Therefore, you bring the whole of you to the table. When you bring 100% of you (having done the work that I take my clients through to get there) and she brings 100% of her to the table, that is when the king meets his queen. He stands alone in his power and she stands alone in her power and side by side they are formidable because they grow exponentially together while both taking radical responsibility for themselves.

This is a beautiful dance of her *choosing* to surrender in her power to her King, knowing and trusting that he has developed the muscle to listen, act and assert his gut instinct for the greater good of all! Now that is what I call a power couple. This is the couple who, when they walk into a room, you feel their presence. There is something about them, an energy that you can't quite put your finger on. They move a certain way together and individually they are whole and complete. It's not about the clothes, watches or handbags they wear but more about who they 'be' when they walk in the room. The royalty have arrived not because they were born into it but because they chose to do the work for themselves and have earned their respect. Cue the royals.

The Final Phase - The Elder.

We all know an elder; he is in his seventies and is a man not concerned with status. He is grounded and everyone comes to him for advice. He is so comfortable pottering around his home, crafting and nurturing the things he loves to do. This phase is for him and who he chooses to let in.

Not every man reaches this stage nor do they want it. The numbers get smaller and smaller the further up the stages we grow. We all know a man at this stage. He is the head of the family. I know one elder in my life and he is my father-in-law.

He is one of eight siblings. He is not the oldest but the middle child. He is in his late seventies to be 80 next year. He lives humbly in the same home he has lived in for 47 years, a two-up two-down end terrace that was extended into a four bedroomed home when his sons were in their teens. He has several times been offered a bigger and better property in a more prestigious area. Yet he refuses because he is happy with his home, his neighbours and community. His neighbours tend to his garden and look after the home when he spends his winters in Spain. He will never leave that home despite having two multi-millionaire sons. In fact, his granddaughters say there is only one way grandad and grandma will leave that home - in a box!

The quality of life that he chooses to live and the joy he finds in the small things in life are what inspire others to seek his wisdom and advice. Whenever there is a problem in the community they come to him and he sits them down at his extendable dining table over a home cooked meal made with love by my mother-in-law, and they talk. He has a way of listening with love and then guiding in a selfless direction with an open heart. He doesn't ask nor seek people to come to him but there is a sense his door is always open. He is happy alone and happy to help but does not need it. This is the village elder.

What follows next are some exploratory questions to help you deepen this work and help you understand you!

Please take your time, where you won't be disturbed and reflect and write in here your thoughts and answers.

Notice which of the 4 decision centres you are answering from?

I am specifically asking you about feelings and for some of you this will be hard for you to access straight away, because it is unfamiliar and takes practice. The reason I ask about feelings is because they are the gateway to change. Think Ferrari, you don't buy a Ferrari because it is logical, you buy one because of the way it makes you feel. Hence, me asking you to access your feelings so you can unlock the key to your truth - the path to freedom.

Finally, a tip on how to assess your feelings - don't try and think about it and rush to the first answer. Accessing feelings for a man requires you to dig deep into your heart and the pit of your stomach. that takes time for you to process. So just sit quietly with your eyes closed, ask the question, be patient and the feelings will reveal themselves usually in a whisper.

1. The question is, which phase are you currently in?

(TIP: Most men put themselves in the phase above where they really are especially high achievers. It comes from the Ego decision centre not the heart. I advise you to close your eyes and take 3 deep breaths: this has been proven to provide heart and brain coherence so you can access information from the heart

and remove the ego to access the truth. Then ask the question again and wait for your heart guided answer. Ego is designed to keep us safe, heart is designed to provide the truth to set you free!)

2. Are you able to honour it now without judging or justifying yourself?

If yes, fantastic! If no, write down here why? What stories and judgement is coming up for you?

Then ask yourself, are these really true?

If this was your friend saying this to themselves what would you say to him?

3. Is this something you can navigate and explain to your partner (if you don't have one think of your last partner, could you have shared this with her)?

If yes, great, do it or offer to share this chapter with them.

If not, what is holding you back? Notice and write down what emotions come up for you?

Are these emotions your default? Do they help you or hinder you?

4. How does understanding these phases make you feel? Lighter? Heavier? Relief? Confused? Happy? Sad? Disappointed? Angry? Clarity? Respect?

5. What positive lessons have you learned in each phase?

6. How have they supported you in your life?

7. Who have you become as a result of each phase?

8. What evidence do you have in your life that these lessons have contributed to your current success?

9. Can you feel gratitude for each phase and the lessons they provided?

10. What lessons can you take into your next phase?

It's important you give yourself time to sit and absorb this information. Reread the chapter. It's a big one and a lot to digest.

Give yourself permission to be ok with where you are at and maybe reflect on the lessons you have learnt in each phase.

In the next chapter I am going to take a deep dive into the tunnel. The reason for this is because most men spend the longest time in this area and is where most of my clients are and where the real growth occurs.

66

'FEEL YOUR SUFFERING, REST
WITH IT, EMBRACE IT, MAKE LOVE
WITH IT. FEEL YOUR SUFFERING
SO DEEPLY AND THOROUGHLY
THAT YOU PENETRATE IT, AND
REALIZE IT'S FEARFUL
FOUNDATION.'

David Deida

5

THE TUNNEL

We talked in the last chapter about the different stages of the life of a man and where the tunnel fits in, and so in this chapter I want to focus solely on the tunnel, what it is, its impact on men and then the relationship – that is, the woman. The reason I am working in this area is because this is the most important stage. If you can master and navigate through. you reach a level of peace and acceptance that is worth way more than the billions you may or may not have in the bank. This chapter is the reason men work with me and pay me six figures to solve this problem. It's the one that moves the needle in all areas of their lives - finances, relationship, family, everything.

Firstly, why is it called the tunnel?

When men talk about this experience, that is what they describe, a long dark place where they believe there is light at the end of it but are unsure of how to get there or if they ever will. It is a literal description.

What is the tunnel? And why?

I touched on this in the previous chapter and I think it is worth digging deeper because that is where the gold is and the roadmap to navigating your way out.

The tunnel is identified by men usually 45 and above. These men have worked hard all their lives to build wealth, what they believed to be the gateway to freedom and fulfilment. The truth is though, while the wealth has given them access to so many opportunities: travel, experiences, achievements, accolades, possibly fame and fortune, it has not provided them with the feeling of success and fulfilment. This is the missing piece of the jigsaw for them. The puzzling and soul-destroying part for them. Imagine sacrificing family, fun and joy to put the long hours in to do what it takes for most of your adult life, and to be left with this dark place of feeling lost and abandonment, asking yourself the questions:

Was it worth it?

What am I on this earth for?

What is the point?

Why do I feel like it is never enough?

I have everything but happiness and satisfaction?

These questions are real tunnel questions. If you have been asking yourself these questions, it is very likely you are in the depth of the tunnel. Just knowing this, I have found, has given men a sense of relief that they are not alone or going mad. The next question I get asked is, *How long does it last?*

It depends on many factors.

Your awareness?

Your ability to take radical responsibility for your life?

Your elasticity to grow?

Your support, including your partner in life?

Your emotional intelligence?

Who is running the show - ego, head, heart or dick?

How badly do you want to pass through?

How willing are you to accept where you are now and not fight?

This is not an easy topic nor should it be rushed through, a bit like the tunnel itself. It is designed to be a process rather than an end point, which for most driven, successful men is very difficult to comprehend. There is a fundamental difference between most men and women and that is men tend to do things to get to the end goal and need it to be done in the most efficient and effective way, taking the least amount of time. Whereas if you ask a woman, it's about the journey, the process, not about getting from a to b. Although that matters it is not as important as the learning and experience on the way. I am referring to personal relationships and not work place for the context of this conversation.

What the tunnel does is provide men with an opportunity to understand the value of the process and it can only do this by creating obstacles on the way - like feelings of loss, frustration. It's in the discomfort that we feel the urge to move and seek new answers.

This is so important if you are going to reach Kinghood. Imagine a king without these skills to navigate the war. They have to experience a war within in order to navigate one without. The tunnel provided a period of apprenticeship to really experience what it takes to find humility, respect and peace from within, when most of your time has been spent sourcing it from your environment - homes, luxury life, partners, cars, and so on.

The tunnel helps you find your inner game solutions.

Unfortunately, many men die in the tunnel, but the 1% like you who seek the truth in books like this, and in coaching to dig even deeper in quantum time, are the ones who experience the light, the joy, the peace and freedom of being a king at the end of the tunnel.

This is a journey of self not others.

Let me illustrate. I was working with a very successful entrepreneur, let's call him John. This beautiful multi-millionaire had it all. The private jets, the homes on three continents. He was a guy that had it all on paper but day-to-day he was stressed, struggled with the anxiety of losing it all, and it resulted in him working every minute of every day. He micromanaged his PA and never really trusted anyone, because all people take him for a ride and they can't be trusted. He was in his fifties, a good-looking guy, well-dressed and you felt his presence when he walked in a room. Get the picture?

Week after week he would come to me with questions like:

Why did they do that?

Why do they let you down?

How can people treat me this way?

I have done nothing but be a good friend.

Why is she doing this to me? I have done everything for her.

These are all questions a man at the beginning of the tunnel would ask. Most men never move out of this phase - I call this the blame game phase. Let me interject in John's story to explain the three phases of the tunnel.

I have come to realise while working with men that there are indeed three phases of the tunnel. This area is so complex and navigating this with my clients is the work, because many coaches will guide the path they have determined as the fast track.

What I have found in the past is that when I have done that it has never been the long-term solution. Think of someone telling you which road to take home and they have never been to your home. Finding the light at the end of the tunnel feels like going home. Your home, not anyone else's. So no one else can tell you the path home. Your soul knows its own path, it has just forgotten and needs the human experience of feeling the road underfoot - to establish the way back home. Each step taken on this path in the wrong or right direction is a step closer to all the lessons needed to be learnt as each stone, grain of sand and boulder is felt.

As a coach I am simply a guide to help navigate and reduce the impact of the ride, making it as beautiful an experience as possible and providing you with the support that I believe you can make it and that I have given other great men many times. It is possible for you too in this lifetime. In fact, in quantum time if you are willing to take that ride. I will touch on what quantum time is later.

The Three Phases of the Tunnel

I will attempt to describe them as simply and briefly as possible here but please note this area could be another book in itself.

1. Victim - the blame game; they constantly believe everyone is out to get them. They live in a place of not enough, fear of losing love, money and respect. During this period they are still fighting the world for doing them wrong. They are unable to see a clear solution to the path of fulfilment and feel very frustrated and angry at the world. It is a time of volatile reactions and reactive behaviour. Usually a time known as 'mid-life crisis' or 'male menopause', it is a time when a man feels so frustrated and out of control with his feelings that he tries to change everything in his outer environment. He may divorce his wife of decades, buy a flash sports car, start dating women half his age. All this in a bid to find the feeling of success and fulfilment and validation from the outside world. A sense of belonging.

2. Transition - men are confused because they start to realise that the reality that they have lived all their lives may not be the truth. The beliefs they formed from their parents and upbringing may not be true. They start to question the source of all their information. They start to question their own behaviour and who they really are and what they stand for. They realise that all the decisions they made in phase 1 were made for the wrong reasons. They start to become aware of the real problem and not the one they have focused on in the past.

They are transitioning from,

'How can I prove my worth to the world with my possessions and the people around me?' to 'How can I prove who I am to ME.'

This is a huge shift and the fact that you are reading this right now tells me you are ready to receive this information without being triggered. And if you are being triggered, that is good; it means you are about to grow. Welcome the uncomfortableness. Let's face it: if you were comfortable you wouldn't even be reading this because you wouldn't be hunting for answers. This is the phase I get so excited for because I know that this is the purpose of the tunnel, the period when most pain and growth is felt - a duality that not only strengthens the man but expands the soul. It is so powerful and it is all preparation for the final phase - enlightenment. This is a period of great contemplation and is a very painful time. It requires a lot of courage to walk this path. However, if you have the insight to stick with it and weather the storm, you come out with the greatest gift - Humility at a level you have never experienced.

3. Enlightened - this is the most important part where they start to see the light. This is the phase of radical self-responsibility. This is when the questions change from,

'Why are they doing that to me?' to 'What did I do to cause that and what did I learn?'

There is a distinct energy shift from being powerless in phase one to regaining their power in this phase. Understand the power that you have a choice as to how you behave and respond to the world. She can't make you feel anything. Only if you give her the power does she take control over you. Being the catalyst to witnessing a man claim his power and watching that light bulb switch on is truly a privilege. And once he feels his power he is so magnetising to the opposite sex. It is like he has reclaimed his weapon, his manhood. He is strong and erect. It oozes sensual masculinity. In further chapters I will cover in more depth the masculine and feminine energies and the dance between the two.

The next question is: **Why do men have to endure the tunnel?**

Think back to when you were a child and to the superheroes that you aspired to be like? Maybe it was Batman, Superman or Captain America? Why did you want to be them? What was it about them that attracted you to them?

It was the fact that they daily overcame evil to save the heroine and civilians. They faced adversity and wrongdoing to become the heroes. They did what it takes. Think about those values and beliefs - bravery, strength, tenacity, doing what it takes, fighting good over bad. Fighting for truth, honour and justice.

None of these skills, beliefs and values can be developed in comfort and safety. They have to be developed through adversity. You can't grow a muscle if you don't tear it first.

The tunnel is a man's journey to his super 'heroness.' It's the roadmap to the ultimate battlefield and victory! The war within himself. If he can master himself and save himself, going from victim to victor of his own mind, body and spirit then he becomes the ultimate hero. He becomes the master of himself and if he can master himself then he can save any woman, man or child. This is the power of a true king. He is strong yet gentle. He is calm when others are fierce. He is brave when others are cowards. He is solid when others are weak. Does he feel all those dualities like other men? Hell yes, but the difference between a man who has come through the tunnel and man that has not is that the king knows how to navigate those dualities inside of him and has mastered the art of knowing themselves for the greater good of all. He has the experience to understand the pitfalls, which road to take and how to become the hero much faster. Not because he wants to be the hero but because he has a 'knowingness' that is who he is. It is a sense of 'beingness.' A grace that holds humility and strength all at once.

All this can only be achieved if Mother Nature provides a battlefield that is worthy of a king - hence the tunnel was born. It has been there for centuries first physically, through hunting and war of the tribes. Survival of the fittest. And now in the modern world through navigating this part of a man's life during his path through the tunnel. The tunnel not only provides the battlefield but it also provides the personal battle-field for you to become your own unique hero. You become your own hero first. This being the ultimate achievement, because any other battle after that becomes possible, including the wife.

Now there is another layer to this for entrepreneurs and so in the next chapter I want to discuss the beast that is an entrepreneur, including some of the special qualities that an entrepreneur has in his DNA.

66

'CHOOSING THIS CAREER PATH IS
COMPLETELY IRRATIONAL
BECAUSE THE ODDS OF
SUCCEEDING ARE DISMAL, BUT
MOST SUCCEED BECAUSE OF
THEIR UNWAVERING BELIEF,
LASER FOCUS ON DELIVERING
AND PERSISTENCE.'

Forbes

6

THE ENTREPRENEUR

I have included this chapter because I have found that most financially wealthy men are entrepreneurial, irrespective of their vocation. I have seen doctors, scientists, IT geniuses and business men all display the values, beliefs and behaviours of the beast that is known as the entrepreneur. Before I do, I want you to know that these are my observations, having lived with one for 31 years and worked with and interviewed thousands of men over the years. You start to pick up on traits and patterns that are unique to them. The reason I am taking the time to explain this is because understanding and becoming aware of these characteristics not only helps the man feel empowered and not alone, but helps his intimate partner appreciate the magic that has to be present in order to achieve magic!

These characteristics are the very reason I call my husband Mr Magic. Mr Magic truly arrived from understanding the BEAST known as 'The Entrepreneur'.

This Beast is so different from any other man. I actually only discovered this when I realised that my man was very different from my friends' husbands who weren't entrepreneurial.

I want you to know there is no judgement here. There is no wrong or right, just facts.

My friends who were married to men who worked for others didn't have the same traits, which I will discuss later. The characteristics of the beast.

Slowly, as you will probably experience, our friend circles started to evolve to more entrepreneurial couples as I worked more and more with male entrepreneurs. It was then that these traits started to become apparent.

So why is it important to understand the characteristics of the beast? What is the point?

Well, when you can fully understand these traits, it is from this observation that you can strategise intellectually. You can lead with insights into your behaviour and its impact on you and your relationship, finally allowing you to resolve, reset and review.

Before I dive into the five characteristics, I explain them and also provide a light and dark side of each characteristic. What do I mean? Well, with each characteristic I have found that understanding both sides of it helped me process the benefits (light side) to being with the beast and also where we needed to give each other grace (dark side). Just knowing this was super helpful in our marriage.

Also it is helpful to note that you are getting a female perspective as a bonus. I encourage you to read this with two lens in mind, yours and hers.

Let's dive straight into what these characteristics are:

1. Tenacity and focus- the ability to believe in the impossible and do what it takes to make it work, even when everyone else around you doesn't believe it is possible. I remember a client telling me about a business deal that he was working on when everyone else around him said *don't back that person.* I mean everyone; his family, his wife, all his current clients. He continued to work on it for ten years because he believed in it. Now was it the lost time on that deal, no because the value in what he learnt was priceless and as a result of that he went on to make millions and help others in the process.

He was in it for the long game, knowing and trusting his inner gut that it was right for him, others and the greater good of all. Now that is the tenacity I am referring to. The type that keeps going even when it makes no sense and they can't see the light at the end of the tunnel yet. They trust the beast within them that it will be ok.

The light side - is achieving results against all odds even if the results achieved aren't monetary. They see value in experience and knowledge gained as a result.

Dark side - not knowing when to give up and spending a lot of energy and effort that can be directed towards more fruitful results.

2. Obsessive attention to order - having to have order in certain areas of your environment. This could manifest as having to have all the same hangers for your shirts and them being colour coordinated or having to unpack the moment you step in the home from travelling. When speaking to several entrepreneurs they revealed that this was because there is such focus on the task that anything outside of the task that isn't in order creates chaos and that is a big distraction. Before I knew this I couldn't understand the point of all the buttons of his shirts needing to be buttoned on the hangers. It made no sense. Surely it would save time undoing the buttons each time he wanted to wear the shirt? But the chaos in his mind meant that he was distracted by the disorder and therefore it took more time.

The light side - is action, action, action - things got done because of the reduction in distraction therefore providing room for intense focus.

Dark side - unable to let go if it isn't perfectly in order, creating inflexibility. This can literally cause anxiety in their bodies. I wished I had known this because it would have saved us hours of arguments.

3. Hyperspeed brain - often unable to hear a full sentence without interrupting or completing sentences because of their ability to reach *their* endpoint of the message much faster than others. This is a biggie, gentlemen and is one for you to expand and accommodate and here is why. While appreciating how fast your mind works, in basic human communication if you speed to the end before allowing the person to catch up, two things happen. Firstly, they feel unheard and disrespected. Secondly, you are not a mind reader, you run a very high risk of getting the wrong end of the stick.

If I may provide a reframe here for you. If the outcome of your conversation is to provide a solution to the problem in as fast a time as possible then it is important to know the problem clearly, right? Now the problem from whose perspective? Yours or theirs? I mean whose problem are you trying to solve? Yours or theirs? Theirs, right. Unfortunately, when they don't feel heard you miss the opportunity to hear their problem. This results in you putting a lot of time and effort into solving the problem you think they have, barking up the completely wrong tree and wasting so much time. Instead, pause, put your brain in neutral to hear and then solve their problem. The reframe is that if you want to solve their problem you have to slow down to speed up. I appreciate your patience in taking the time to read that long but necessary explanation.

Light side - reaching your own conclusions in record time.

Dark side - often making assumptions based on your frame of the world, resulting in the other person feeling unheard and a breakdown in rapport and relationship building. Possibly you didn't solve their problem and have wasted your time and effort.

4. Misunderstood as aloof - because the way their brains work means they struggle to see different perspectives unless it is from a credible source. A credible source is defined as someone they trust. This could be a role model who has proven results or a well-respected authority in the field, or a trusted family member who has proven their worth. It could be a partner or wife, though this is often not the case if the relationship is not solid.

Light side - they can't be derailed easily.

Dark side - can be isolating, leaving them feeling lonely and misunderstood.

5. **Generosity** - when they see potential, they will help people above and beyond their duty because they understand relationship equity and the law of reciprocity. I have so many stories of how my husband has been so generous even to the point of paying for a man's mortgage because he had four children and was about to be homeless and not expecting anything back in return. This man years later went on to work with one of the biggest oil companies in the world and provide

my husband with incredible resources and first pick and access to business opportunities that he would never have had. So while the beast struggles with day-to-day relationship communication, they have an inner sixth sense of who the good people are and who is worth supporting unconditionally.

Light side - often pays off in energy exchange of love, loyalty or money.

Dark side - they can be taken advantage of and are often.

You will have noticed I have noted the light and dark side of the beast characteristics. This concept first came to me when I started working and surrounding myself with successful entrepreneurs like my husband.

It wasn't every man that had to have the same hangers for all his shirts and the shirts had to be buttoned all the way down! *I mean, how does that make sense?* You have to unbutton the whole thing to get the shirt off the hanger! Or the fact that chairs or books had to be placed exactly straight, they couldn't be at an angle.

Gentlemen - inside bonus scoop from the female mind - she *doesn't* realise you can't help it - she thinks you are being ridiculous and there are more important things in life than worrying about if a chair is straight.

The reason I explain her point of view is not for you to change but for you to be aware that not everyone has those traits and to give a little grace when she doesn't get it. **Also, it is these very traits that get you to succeed in work.**

However, I once heard a CEO state that it is impossible to succeed and focus on work and also a relationship. I believe that is because once you are focused on something and if that something is your driver to provide £ or $ through work, you will do whatever it takes. Even if that means putting zero attention and focus on the wife!

Ouch! For some of you, that is a very hard pill to swallow. But I encourage you to sit with it.

What is the truth?

Did you invest as much energy into your marriage as you did your business?

And if you had, would you still be married?

No judgement here, just another point of view for you to consider. When we take radical responsibility for our behaviour that is when the transformation can truly happen.

Many of my multi-millionaire clients come to me and say *well, she went off with the 'pool guy' and so she ended the marriage.* It's her fault and yes, I am not condoning extramarital affairs and women are three times more likely to file for divorce than a man. *Or maybe you were the one that strayed because you weren't getting your needs met?*

Either way, if you can consider that if your needs aren't being met that also her needs aren't being provided for?

Often men believe there is only one way to provide and that is financially, but that is just one way. Often the three other ways are overlooked and massively undervalued especially by super-focused entrepreneurs. These three ways are:

1. Focused time - I know you believe you do this and it still isn't enough. I want you to know it's not that you are doing it wrong. It's just not being done in a way that she is registering. There are some very simple and fundamental differences between focused time for a man and women. Let me explain. The key differences are firstly, eye contact - she needs eye contact. Secondly, don't attempt to multitask, you can't, and she will feel it. So no sneakily playing Candy Crush with one hand while rubbing her back. Be 100% committed to her in this time. After all, is she not the most important person in your life? She chooses every day to walk this path with you. She doesn't have to. So give her the dignity of your undivided attention when you say you will. Nothing should be more important than this.

Thirdly, be a man of your word - if you say you are going to commit to 3pm for an hour, show up at 3pm for an hour, not 3.05, or 3.10 and then schedule something at 3.30. Nothing is more important than this sacred time and your word. This is so important because when you honour your word to her and she feels it, it sends her a signal that she can trust you to keep her safe and if she can trust you to keep her safe then she doesn't have to protect herself and so she can relax. This is the result you want: a woman that is so relaxed around you.

2. Emotional and physical support as presence - What does this mean, I hear you say? This is not being physically with her in the same room, pretending to focus on her but thinking about work. She knows and feels you are not fully focused on her. Focused time is more energetic than physical. It requires you to not only be with her physically but to be connected with her emotionally.

How you do this is really simple. You put your focus on your heart and think, 'I will protect you, you are safe,'and send her love to her heart when you are with her. You say very little and you get curious about understanding your wife. Not to scan for the problem, but to relax into the unknown. To genuinely become a student of understanding the wife's point of view. A great exercise for this would be for both of you to sit in front of each other, look each other in the eye and for five mins allow her to just talk. Your job is to just listen to understand her, not justify or defend your position. You are not under attack. This is just her point of view and may be very alien to you. If this is done properly you may be pleasantly surprised at by saying nothing, doing nothing other than giving her your emotional and physical attention at the same time you have gifted her the only gift she will ever truly desire from you - your presence.

3. Anticipating needs - this is a biggie and is often missed. Anticipating her needs is not giving her what you think she needs or what she says she needs in the heat of the moment. I know this is very confusing for men. So let me unpack this in a way that is meaningful to you.

A woman speaks in clues, she expects you to be the detective. Think Inspector Morse. She uses indirect communication which I will explore deeper in the communication chapter. But for now, I will explain in the context of this conversation. Let me give you an example. When she would like you to run her a bath she might say, 'I love hot bubble baths' or when she wants you to invite her on a date, she might say, 'Do you remember how much fun we had the last time you took me on a date?' or if she hasn't developed her emotional intellect it may even sound like, 'You never take me out on a date.'

This is admittedly not the best way to motivate a man, but unfortunately, if she hasn't done the work it will happen. Can you see how it is indirect? You have to look for the clues and then provide if it feels aligned to you without asking her. So for example, surprise her and run a bath or bring her a cup of tea or coffee when she least expects it but you know it's the time she would normally have one. It doesn't have to cost the earth; in fact, it is often the very small things that will make the most impact. It is not about the **money** you spend but the **effort** YOU put in. The thought, the noticing her clues and then remembering and acting on it not because you feel obliged or because she said, but because you want to and it feels aligned for you.

I often hear entrepreneurs when they are on a 'big'' project say, 'I neglect my wife because I can't sustain both, but once the project is over I promise I will make it up to her.' Here is the problem with that. She feels your work is more important than her and always takes priority.

Imagine if she said, 'I will cook you dinner and look after you once I have finished going to the thing that is important to me.' Next week you might get dinner and she stopped taking care of you.

I hear some of you saying she has started doing that already. Ask yourself this question: how long has your 'big' project been going on for? Or does one morph into the next? I remember being promised this and the project just went from one to the next for five years! This left me feeling that I wasn't worthy or a priority of his attention and so I just disconnected. Sad but the honest truth. The return from that was me getting clear on what I needed on a daily basis and being super grateful and appreciative when I received it.

Now there were times when it didn't happen. I learnt not to focus on those times. The reason you're reading this book is to help you learn from my mistakes and it is very possible that your wife is not clear on what she needs. It took me a while to figure this stuff out and so by having the heads up, you get to go first and create your roadmap. Call it your inside scoop to keep her happy. You're welcome. Remember, the key, gentlemen, is to give a little energy and focus to providing these three *daily*. She doesn't want you to do all day but she does want sometime during the day 30-60 minutes solely for her and your relationship daily. Consistency, commitment and focus will breed trust, respect and irresistible animal attraction for you. I promise you, try this for one week and watch the response. I am telling you it will be worth it and could be the very thing that saves your marriage.

In the next chapter I am going to discuss one of the most fundamental reasons most marriages fail. Understanding this gives you a framework on how to identify these problems and fix them before they destroy your marriage.

66

'THE PENTACLE - THE ANCIENTS IN
TWO HALVES - MASCULINE AND
FEMININE. THEIR GODS AND
GODDESSES WORKED TO KEEP A
BALANCE OF POWER. YIN AND YANG.
WHEN MALE AND FEMALE WERE
BALANCED, THERE WAS HARMONY IN
THE WORLD. WHEN THEY WERE
UNBALANCED THERE WAS CHAOS.'

Dan Brown

7

THE MASCULINE AND FEMININE

This chapter is the reason my marriage was failing and the reason it survived. If you read no other chapter but this it could save your marriage. It is the piece of information which, when I reveal to every client, they respond, 'If I had known this twenty years ago I could have saved my marriage!'

What I am about to share with you will make you look at all your female relationships in a completely new light, especially your intimate ones from the past and present, and will influence how you navigate them in the future. I have kept it at this point in the book because I want you to fully understand the power of it so you can really shift the needle in your intimate relationships moving forward. So here goes, are you ready?

I want to share something to illustrate what can go so dramatically wrong when you don't understand this information.

I want to give you a flavour of the imperfections in us all, including the so-called 'expert'. I am going to share a story that is so personal to me and I share it publicly on podcasts (including Tony Robbins' Podcast) as it illustrates a very common problem and solution in marriages . I am not proud of my behaviour but I know it is 'real'; it's 'life'. The point of the story is to help you understand the profound differences between men and women and that nobody is wrong or right, we are all just trying to navigate this crazy world of love and intimacy. Just trying to do our best.

Deep breath, here goes.

It was about seven years into our marriage. We had got over the honeymoon stage of constant sex and excitement. We were at the 'pick your damn socks up' stage. Our first daughter was three years old and we were both focused on our careers and making a better life for us. In my head he was married to his work. Truthfully, I had convinced myself that he was having an affair. Not with another woman but with his work. It seemed like he loved it and would rather wine and dine her than me. Does this sound familiar?

I would say things like:

'I am so sick of you being at work!'

'You love your work more than me.'

'Why can't you get a *real* job like every other man?'

'It is not normal to work eighteen hours.'

'Do we have to have the phone constantly on?'

I could go on and on but you get the idea, right?

The permanent criticism and comparison to much more successful men. Ouch!

The time it took for me to expend all that energy on hate and frustration made me a bitter and resentful woman to live with. I look back with hindsight and wonder why he put up with me.

Life leaves clues. I just didn't have the insight to see them.

I am not saying anyone is right or wrong, just that we were both 'asleep' to what was really going on. It's like trying to drive a car and never being taught not only how to drive but what the gears or the steering wheel or any other part of the car's function is.

Here is what I have lived through and coached many couples through. It's a pattern I have seen over and over again and that is the depolarisation of a relationship. It is spoken of by many great experts in this space, Ester Perel, David Deida, Tony Robbins and many more.

Before I explain depolarisation I need to explain the masculine and feminine energies and what they mean.

This concept was the reason my marriage was failing and the understanding of it is the reason we celebrated our 26th wedding anniversary. I have used this information with every single client I have worked with and it has blown their minds at how powerful it is and how much sense it makes. It is one of those things that once you have heard it you can't unhear it. There is no going back. It is the reason why the sex and passion stops or becomes functional in a relationship and the solution to it becoming explosive. It is possible to reignite your marriage with this information.

Do I have your attention now?

I want to introduce to you the concept of masculine and feminine **energies.** I am not talking about men and women but the energies we all have in us.

Let's start with defining what masculine and feminine energies are. They have been described as a list of characteristics that we all have. I have masculine energies in me, and if you are a man you will have feminine in you. It is not a bad thing, it is just the beautiful balance of polarity within you. Let's clarify - we all have both energies and we all have our own unique sweet spot of balance. For example, when I am balanced I am 80% feminine and 20% masculine. This is when I feel the most aligned.

Here was the problem: for the second decade of my marriage I was operating at 80% masculine and 20% feminine, totally out of balance. I was angry, frustrated, even depressed and had chronic pain in my neck that the doctors couldn't explain. It wasn't until I addressed my energy balance that this pain left my body. When I did, it was literally in seconds. It was like a veil had been lifted and I could finally see myself. I am not saying all women's balance is 80% feminine and 20% masculine. There is no magic number. Most men have a higher masculine side than feminine and according to David Deida, an expert in this space, 80% of men have a high masculine balance.

Now the key is to firstly identify what that looks like for you, before we can even touch on the impact of these energies in relationships. They are literally the difference between your marriage surviving or not and is probably the reason why you ended the relationship of your dreams.

Let me tell you how I learnt I was way off balance. It was the day I found myself in Maui at a Tony Robbins' Platinum Partners event. I had dragged my hubby of 22 years halfway around the world because *he needed fixing*. He was the problem because I was the coach and I was 'bloody perfect', right!

I couldn't have been more wrong. Firstly, this beautiful man had not wanted to come to a Tony Robbins event. He didn't even know who he was. I don't know if you are familiar with Tony's work or have been to one of his events. If you haven't, I would highly recommend you look him up. His events are twelve-hours, non-stop, no pee or food breaks and you are up dancing and moving for a lot of them over a minimum of 4 days.

To paint the picture, my man is very private and hates being the centre of attention; I on the other hand love being the centre of attention. I am a front row kind of gal and he is a back row observer. I ask a lot of questions and he is more of a listener and observer. So you can imagine his face when we got there. He was supposed to be at his new company's biggest trade show in France at the same time as this event. He had a choice: to let 150 people down or his wife. Did he choose work or love? He chose love; this was lesson one that I missed. This story illustrates how blind we can be to the gifts men give. We get so caught up in our own stories and pain that we can't see the woods from the trees.

We arrive in Maui, and day one Tony addressed the audience and asked, 'Who in the room doesn't want to be here?'

Three people stood up out of a room of 500; my man was one of them. Part of me nearly died as he stood head to shoulder with Tony, who is 6' 7" and another part of me was so proud of this man who stands for what he believes in and doesn't care who that is in front of. He is a real man. This was my first experience of feeling the duality of the masculine and feminine within me.

Tony looked my husband straight in the eye and time stood still. There was an exchange of honour and respect that Tony provided for my man that I had never witnessed before, which blew me away. A level of love between two human beings, unconditionally and so profound. It was truly humbling. Tony said, 'All I ask is that you keep an open mind and you are obviously free to leave whenever you like.' Now because Tony honoured Atul man to man, masculine energy to masculine energy, Atul said, 'Ok, I can do that.'

And so day one continued. We enjoyed most of it until Atul said he was tired and going to bed. He didn't want to party with all my 'platinum partner' friends. It was traditional that we all party after each day. I was horrified that he wanted to go to bed. I mean, he had only been in six different time zones in the last 72 hours. When I look back now, I can see this in a completely different light.

So anyhow he was totally antisocial and didn't care about my friends and therefore me. As I write this I have mixed emotions of disappointment, sadness and sorrow for what I didn't see. The blind spots that we all experience. The darkness that we believe to be real. The pain that we suffer and blame on others. The faith that someone else will be our saviour. Oh, how I was wrong.

We had the biggest fight that evening and in my usual predictable way I blamed him for everything and he took it because he was exhausted. The next day we were at a relationship event in Maui, one of my bucket list destinations, but I couldn't see, hear or feel any of it. I was so angry and frustrated and totally in my head. I had already planned the divorce and how we were over. I had made the biggest drama and he was the villain. Now I am not saying he was all innocent and I was all to blame, but what I am saying is that I had allowed myself to become the victim of my own mess and was blaming it on him

This had been a pattern I had formulated all my life as a way to protect myself. It was a defence mechanism. I will hurt you before you hurt me, when the truth is I was hurting both of us in the pursuit to protect. I had lost all sight of the reason we were married and why we chose each other - LOVE. I was consumed in being right. In being the one who was perfect and didn't need to do any work. It was all him, the way he walked, talked and even breathed. It was an awful mess.

I then proceeded to spend the day punishing him by ignoring him, sitting in the front row with my friends and telling him to sit at the back. I was literally the bitch from hell when I look back. He spent the day trying to console me and make up. I wasn't having any of it and made everyone, including Tony, perfectly aware. At 10.30pm at night, Tony was sitting at the back of the room as we had just finished hearing Ester Peril speak on Zoom, an incredible leader in the relationship space, and I stood up on the front row and made a comment.

Now I was feeling fairly self-righteous and confident that I was right. But you know when you say something and the moment it leaves your mouth you realise it was the wrong thing to say! The energy in the room dropped; you could cut the atmosphere with a knife. Then it happened. I felt this huge energy come from the back of the room. It was Tony. He bellowed from the back, 'Where is Dimple!!' It was the loudest roar I have ever felt in my life. Every bone in my body shook. Then it happened, FI, FIE, FOE, FUM; his huge size 19 shoes pounded down the aisle; he was coming for me. It was like everything became slow motion; time almost stood still.

I remember standing up, all 5' 2" of me as the hairs on the back of my very short-shaved haircut stood to attention. He came straight for me. I was the target. He stopped about thirty centimetres from me and his 6' 7" frame towered over me. Then it began. He was so fierce that many of his platinum partners who had followed him for fifteen years said they had never felt him that angry before. He was pissed. I want to point out that there was never a time that I felt intimidated or threatened by Tony because I felt the integrity of his heart. He was matching my masculine energy with the same masculine power I was projecting. He was mirroring me very cleverly but on the outside it looked fierce.

Now came the drop the mic, biggest light bulb moment.

It was when my beautiful man came from nowhere, with his chest puffed out making him grow 2 inches, with the most focused and fiercest look on his face. He was ready to go to war, attack, not me but the 6ft 7" giant. Now just to clarify my man is 6Ft, so he is not a small man but Tony Robbins would dwarf any man. Here was the pivotal moment that changed everything. the light bulb moment. It took for Tony Robbins to stop what he was doing with me, turn and face Atul and say, ' Is this the man you are talking about not forgiving?' He put his arm around him and said, ' I fucking love this brother he has shown more courage today than you have ever shown in your life! He has come here to take me down to protect you because nobody talks to his women like that.' Now bear in mind we were heading for a divorce, I had been the bitch from hell, wife all day and he still (I had to take a deep breath as I write this because it still makes me tear up 4 years to the day later) came to my rescue. Here was the lesson for me, *I didn't notice him come to protect me! It took for Tony Robbins to make me really see him and his effort.*

The very thing I had been desperately seeking was right under my nose, but because I was too busy focusing on the lack and not on what I had, I had completely missed it. The very thing I was so desperate for protection and to feel safe had always been there. I had just never seen it. Resulting in me feeling unsafe and needing to protect myself. And the only way I could achieve that was in the masculine energy.

The intervention went on for two hours, with me going down on my knees to beg for forgiveness from my husband for the appalling way I had behaved and my husband meeting me on his knees and us healing our marriage that day.

The reason I tell this story is to give you context to the masculine and feminine and how they can create havoc if out of balance! Can any of you relate to any part of this story?

Whether you can or can't, this concept is fundamental for anyone who wants a healthy relationship. For the purposes of this book I will give you an introduction. For further information, reach out to my team or the abundance of resources I have available, from self-learning to one to one coaching.

Now let's unpack the story, explain the masculine and feminine energies, and how they impact most long-term relationships.

In the beginning there is a massive attraction because of the polarity. Polarity is when you have opposite core energies, just like a magnet's negative and positive charge means the magnets pull each other together, but if you have positive and positive or even negative and negative the magnets repel each other. Humans are the same, otherwise we depolarise each other. In the beginning of most relationships;

The Honeymoon Stage

Usually the woman is in her natural core feminine and the man is in his natural core masculine. For same sex couples, usually one is naturally more masculine and the other is more feminine. If you are not sure which you are, I will explain the characteristics a bit later. For now I want you to understand why relationships fall apart and how you can heal them back to magic and the ultimate intimacy.

Let's go back to the honeymoon stage - there is polarity, the passion is there and the attraction is there and everyone is happy, especially because usually at the beginning we are operating in our authentic core energy. We aren't faking it and physical intimacy is magic.Then it happens:

The Depolarisation Stage

The relationship develops, marriage and children usually, and there is a shift that looks like a lack of intimacy, fighting, irritation and competition. These are signs of depolarisation; that is, they are repelling each other. This usually happens because the woman has shifted into her inauthentic masculine totally unconsciously, usually as a result of having children and or a high-flying career. She is going into protection mode. Especially if she is married to an entrepreneur due to their characteristics discussed in a previous chapter.

This is exactly what happened to me - he was nowhere to be seen, working all hours, I was at home with a newborn. I didn't feel safe or protected and the only way I knew how to protect myself was to become the man and rise in my masculine. Except the problem was there was already a masculine man in the relationship. Life became a competition and we would constantly fight. We were both miserable. This was the phase when he would rather be at work than come home. The constant criticism and controlling behaviour became too much for him.

Does this sound familiar? This went on for ten years in my marriage before the next stage.

The Demasculation Stage

I call this the losing yourself or demasculation or handing over your balls phase. This is where the masculine man is so fatigued and his desire to keep her happy is so strong, that one of three things happens:

1. He settles - drops into his feminine and becomes a 'yes' boy! Yuck - totally demasculating, very unattractive. The reason this happens is twofold - he wants the path of least resistance and therefore effort, and he wants sex and the only way that happens is if there is polarisation even if it is inauthentic. He responds to his inauthentic masculine woman and becomes inauthentic feminine. False polarity equals sex but it's not authentic polarity so what happens is the sex is vanilla. scratch an itch kind of sex. You become room-mates with French benefits.

2. He strays - because his sexual, connection and honour needs are not being met in the home and his desire to feel like a man is so strong that he seeks respect, honour and sex elsewhere.

3. He separates - divorce because he can't see another solution and she is also tired and exhausted with the lack of connection. Nobody's needs are being met and both people end up blaming the other and/or he blames himself for failing to keep his woman happy, and he moves on to the next marriage and make the same mistake. He doesn't realise that it is not either person's fault but simply depolarisation and then inauthentic polarisation.

Let me explain what is happening in most marriages and how this concept is responsible for a lot of the problems and the failed marriages. I believe that if we were taught this in high school we would half the divorce rate.

Here is what is happening in a nutshell. In the beginning there is so much passion, attraction, sex and intimacy that I call this the honeymoon phase. This is when the polarity is very high and so attraction is high. This phase can last up to seven years and is beautiful and fun. Then either work or children or both come along and the relationship becomes work. This is the struggle phase. The relationship becomes depolarised. The sex is terrible or non-existent and work or children are blamed for it; the truth is that it's the depolarisation of the relationship.

Finally, there is a secret fourth S and that is **solve** and is a very simple but effortful piece of work. However, once you have this nailed, your relationships will never be the same. It reaches a level of deep understanding and passion on a soul, heart and physical level. It is beautiful and too extensive to cover in this book. That is for another book and for my executive coaching clients.

I suspect you are wondering what the characteristics of masculine and feminine energy are and how you can identify which you are. I expect you also want to know how to attract the opposite in your partner to maintain polarisation, because that is really the name of the game in relationships. Authentic Polarisation.

I have you covered in this. I am going to discuss the basics with you in the next chapter as this will also be the foundation for understanding how to communicate with the opposite sex. It is a bloody good chapter. Buckle up, you are in for a ride.

66

"WHEN PEOPLE TALK, LISTEN
COMPLETELY. MOST PEOPLE
NEVER LISTEN."

Ernest Hemingway

8

RELATIONSHIPS AND COMMUNICATION

I n this chapter I am going to cover the most fundamental victor and victim of relationships. It is the thing that makes or breaks a relationship. It is the combination of understanding the dualities of energy and the sexes that will provide a clear roadmap on how we communicate with the opposite sex.

Before I dive in, I want you to think back to the hundreds of arguments that you had with your partner/s and I can guarantee it went something like this:

Her: You are not listening to me! You don't understand me!

Him: I heard everything you said. Why are you so mad about the toilet seat? It's no big deal. I promise you, I will remember.

Her: You don't care about me. If you did you would remember without me having to ask you. You never listen, you just don't care.

Him: I do care; look at everything else I do for you! You don't appreciate anything I do. I told you I am sorry! Why can't you just drop it? I am so tired of this BS.

Her: Because you never learn or listen!

It may not be about the toilet seat but you get the idea. We find ourselves repeating the same patterns over and over again. Leaving him feeling lost, confused and tired and her feeling misunderstood, unheard and scared. None of which is true. It all boils down to a lack of understanding of how we need to be communicated to depending on which energy we are in.

In this chapter I am going to give you some gold on how to navigate this and real actionable things you can do to never have those conversations. This sounds simple and it is, because once you know it, you can't undo it. It is impossible to go back.

The first thing to understand is that the energy you are operating in will determine your style, goal and point of communication. In the table below I have illustrated very briefly and as simply as possible the characteristics of the masculine and feminine energy. The point of this table is to understand why your feminine woman says the things she does and why you communicate the way you do. It's to give you a foundation of knowledge about the differences between men and women.

The comparison between Masculine and Feminine Energies:

Characteristic	Masculine (80% of men)	Feminine (80% of women)
Communication style	Direct	Indirect
Language type	Logical and focused	Illogical and unfocused
Source information	Facts and data	Feels and stories
Direction of movement	Forward and seeking	Leaning back and magnetising
Type of action	Seeking and hunting for answers	Magnetising and drawing the answers to them
Movement	Straight and forward	Flowing and directionless
Thought process	Logical and goal orientated	Free spirited and directionless
Power point	Strategy and skill	Trust and surrendering
needs	Problem solving	Attention and being seen
Expression controls	Head and thinking	Feeling and heart
Motivation	Physical evidence of success	Confidence in instinct/intuition
Connection	Doing and action	Being and sharing

We have both energies inside us and we move from one to the other depending on our environment. We tend to have an authentic preference. The key is to identify your preference and spend most of your time in that energy.

So how do you know what your preference is? To find out by doing a fun quiz, go to https://www.dimpleglobal.com/masculine-feminine-which-are-you/ where you can access the quiz to identify your authentic energy.

Once you have understood this, the next step is to ask yourself whether you happy in this state I know I was miserable in my masculine. I had pain in my neck. I would be stressed all the time and that was all down to me operating in logic and direct communication as opposed to leaning back, allowing things to come to me and feeling into things rather than forcing through doing.

The quiz will not only help you identify where you are now but also if this is where you are happy. If not, change it. You can start by living your life in your preferred energy. For me that was being rather than doing, trusting and leaning back rather than pushing forwards and forcing.

Now you understand the energies it is time to relate that to communication styles. This is a very complex area and so I aim to simplify it by being general. Therefore, this will be true for most but not everyone. There are always going to be exceptions to the rule but for the purposes of this book I am going to teach the general rules between men and women, bearing in mind that 80% of women are happiest in their feminine and 80% of men are happiest in their masculine.

Ok, so ladies first. Let's look first at women. I know this is the biggest question men ask - how do I communicate to a woman?

The first thing is not about what you say but what you are expecting. When you talk to a woman most men expect them to respond like a man and this is impossible. You are setting yourselves up for failure. When you assume a woman is going to reply with logic you are doomed. We can't give you a straight answer when we are in feminine flow because we operate on feelings, not facts.

For example, the other day my husband asked me a question, 'Do you want chips or mashed potatoes?' Now the logical answer would be to choose chips or potatoes, right? But what I answered was, 'What do you want?'

My feminine brain was trying to establish a connection with him, so I asked, "what do you *feel* like having? and then depending on what I *felt* like I would either connect with him on the same *feeling* about the type of potatoes or not. It would depend on how I was *feeling*. It is not straight forward for the feminine. There is a lot to consider. Guys, there are a lot of scenarios that go on in our heads. A lot. It drives us crazy sometimes and most women aren't even aware it is happening!

The moral of this story is to expect an illogical answer and don't judge it or get frustrated. In fact, honour it because the feeling of connection that she constantly makes with you is the same feeling of connection that you desire. Her route to it is just different from yours. If you can just recognise it as that, your life and hers will be a lot easier because you will expect an indirect response and find it endearing because of her desire to connect with you. I know what you are thinking. 'how the hell did he know what type of potatoes I wanted?' Here is how he told me what he wanted and then I told him my preference. I needed the journey of connection first before I got to the end point.

The second thing to note is that it's not about getting to the point with her. I hear you saying, well what is the point of the conversation then?

Here is the gold, guys. The difference between the purpose of the conversation for men and women is this:

Men talk to get to the end of the journey; women talk to experience the journey. Imagine a conversation is like a road trip and you type in your postcode or zip code and you set your target, hit the fastest route. Now that is how a man would navigate his conversation - end in mind and in as few words as necessary. Women, on the other hand, may not even type in the zip code or postcode. She might just decide to drive and see where the road takes her. Her experience is about feeling the adventure and noticing everything on the way.

If you say to her after twenty minutes of conversation which feels like going around the houses (because in her mind that is what she is doing), 'Can you get to the point?' she will often look confused. There is no end point. She just needs you to enjoy her experience with her.

This is the fundamental reason she may repeat things over and over again. If she feels your frustration or impatience during this process it will cause her to start all over again because the point of this conversation for her is not the end point but you *feeling* what she is feeling and experiencing.

She wants you to go on the journey with her. That is how you connect with her and light her up and in turn it will light you up. Let go of the end point and focus on understanding what she is feeling. It is not about the facts but the story and how it makes her feel. I must stress - and this is so gold so listen carefully - if you interrupt a woman mid story to correct her with the 'facts' because her version of the story is not true she will feel disrespected and will shut you down even if you are right. And here is why. She is telling the story to convey a feeling and her perception of the facts and correcting her is like someone telling you that your facts are a lie.

Finally, the most important thing to remember when communicating with a woman is not what you say but how you listen. The number one complaint you will hear time and time again from your woman is, 'You are not listening,' even when you can repeat word for word what she said. And that is the problem. She doesn't care if you can repeat her words; her currency is feelings. You may be able to repeat her words but can you repeat how she feels? Here is the true mastery of women. If you can fully engage in a conversation with your woman, say a few words and make her *feel* understood, that will be the game changer for you.

The next question is, how to do it, And here is the answer. It is a really simple process but very few men execute it well. They either rush it or miss a step out or completely forget and go into auto pilot mode and revert back to thinking she is a man and get frustrated when she responds like a woman. Before we continue, I am not asking you to change your style or who you are. I am simply asking you to consider the definition of insanity; that is to keep doing what you do and expect different results. I am asking you to consider that there may be a much more effective and efficient way to spend your efforts and energy, respectively and get a much more desired outcome. A happy woman who honours and respects you and provides you with your needs.

Is it worth trying something new for that?

Here is the formula on how to talk to women:

1. Stop what you are doing. I mean everything. Do not try to multitask, you can't, and she will know even when you are on the phone.
2. Put your brain in neutral. Don't think about anything; have a blank mind.
3. Look at her if she is with you or via video screen (still works) - in the eyes, not stare like a weirdo but softly like you are genuinely curious.
4. Get curious about searching NOT for the problem BUT what is she feeling. Listen for the message beneath the words.
5. Focus on understanding her, not the problem; feel compassion and love.
6. Be patient; it may take some time but it will be a lot less time than weeks of hearing the same story over and over again. It will be worth it.

7. You know when she has finished because she will sigh. That is not the time to tell her how to fix her problem. Please resist the temptation to do this, unless she asks for your opinion, because if you do you will have just wasted all your effort. She is not interested in the end point. In fact, she probably knows the solution, she just needs to share the story and her feelings, that is all.

Guys this is my 1.0 communication class. It is the very basics I cover with my clients as a starting point. If you can nail this then you qualify to come work with me. This is the foundation though. So important.

Now that we have covered the basics of communication, in the next few chapters I want to move on to what you believe women want and desire in a relationship. This will be the piece that some of you will find hard to believe.

Get ready.

66

"ALL GREAT ROADS ARE PAVED
WITH UNCOMFORTABLE
MEMORIES."

Amy Neftzger

9

WHY DO YOU KEEP F**ING UP?

I n this chapter I am going to talk to you about the real truth behind what has been going on for years and years in your life and is the reason you have never felt successful in your life despite having all the external things that you love. This chapter is towards the end of the book because it's the biggest pill to swallow and if I had mentioned this at the beginning you probably would not have continued. This is my no BS coaching that is about to occur. I know we are friends now and I trust you can take this blow from a woman, because quite frankly you have nothing to lose other than your ego.

In your business you have probably surrounded yourself with 'yes' men. Everyone arse-licks the boss. They tell you how amazing you are and that every idea you have is a good one, when sometimes they are just bum ideas. Or maybe you have one or two trusted associates or friends who tell you the truth, but you know they hold back for fear of losing you. Either way, the consequence of these patterns of behaviour is that at worst you lose a deal and at best you are successful. No biggie. Yes, there's a little frustration or inconvenience, but you still feel strong and safe within yourself.

Now let's look at matters of the heart - yours first and then how this impacts your woman (past, present or future).

How we navigate certain situations in our life is all determined by our values, our beliefs of ourselves and our abilities in that situation. It's just like you can tell your woman until you are blue in the face that she is not fat and she won't believe you because her belief system is set up to believe she is fat. Nothing you can say will convince her. Well in the same way, you have beliefs about how good you are at business, fatherhood, sex, husbandhood and women. These beliefs usually come from early childhood and from how our parents modelled this in life for us. For example, I believed growing up that all men were unsafe, because I was raised in a home where my first childhood memories were of my mum's blood on the walls as a result of a man.

The reason I am talking about this very basic and common-sense thing is because even though we know our beliefs shape us, how often do we actually sit and identify them and decide that they are what we want?

This my dear gentlemen is the start of the real work, where only 1% dare to go. Why? Because it takes courage to not blame the ex, your parents, your upbringing, the mean things that person said to you or the women who said, 'You were terrible in bed.'

This is the work, the time and energy you use to *really* sit with yourself and not revisit the trauma, the heartache, but to decide what you believed as a result of that. How old were you when you decided that about myself and women? How long has that child been running the show? Is it really true?

I know this is getting deep and some of you want to run at this part. I encourage you to notice the trigger. It's just the little boy scared. He has built up these beliefs over years and never really addressed them. These are deep dark secrets that he may never have spoken of to anyone, including himself. They have been running the show. Things like,

'All women are after my money.'

'I provide everything and it is never good enough.'

'My father was right, I will never be able to hold down a marriage.'

'All women hate men.'

'There are no good women left.'

'I am rubbish in bed.'

'I am shy and I don't know how to approach women.'

'I can't say no to women and so I end up losing myself; it's not worth it.'

'I will always be abandoned and alone.'

Let's look at this. Some, all or none of these may be familiar to you? Whichever way, it is important for you to think about what your beliefs are around yourself, your success in life and therefore how you live my life.

It is important to unblind yourself to these beliefs because:

1. These have been running the show your whole life.
2. They are just stories you made up as a child and believed them to be true - at what age? I bet between five and twelve. For decades you have let a, let's say, seven-year-old decide your worthiness in your personal esteem and relationships.
3. Is this the truth? That story of your parents fighting, or your father telling you you would be no good, or your parents' divorce and you blaming yourself because you were the reason they fought and now you are the cause of all fights? Or the time when your first love told you were terrible at sex and that was your frame for life! Or the first time the woman dated you for your money.

We gather all these stories as evidence, as proof, that our beliefs are true and we ignore all the other evidence of the millions of times the woman said you were amazing in bed, or the hundreds of times your parents would laugh with pride at one of your achievements, or the successful years of marriage.

Even as I write this I feel many of you are arguing with me. Notice you are doing this all the time to convince yourself that it is true: 'I am not worthy of her love; look at her, she is gorgeous.' 'Most women are gold diggers.' It's almost like it is easier for you to deal with the 'bad self-talk.' then it is to deal with the possibility that it may not be true.

Don't beat yourself up. This is human behaviour. It's how our brain keeps us safe. We all have a natural default to be comfortable in the shit because the nice stuff requires you to be brave and believe in something that may not be true.

It's true if you allow it to be. So if you think you are not worthy of her love, then guess what? You are going to spend a lifetime searching for evidence of how she hates you and how you keep messing up. Just so you can stop feeling bad about yourself and have the comfort of being 'right.' As humans we would rather live in the familiar *pain* than the unfamiliar discomfort of the unknown. The unknown here is you considering that you are worthy of her love or whatever your belief is about you. 'I'm not good enough,', 'They are all gold diggers,' and so on.

So here it is, gentlemen, the truth -

You can *decide* to believe in something different, to trust that it is true, gather evidence to support it, and *change your life*.

It is as simple as that. So why do so many men not do this when it comes to themselves and relationships?

That answer is really easy. It takes courage and balls to stop being a victim of life and to decide to take full responsibility for everything that has happened to your life. Yes, everything. From choosing the family you were born into. The experiences your soul chose to learn from. The heart ache and cruelty you endured. Everything. You chose it. I chose all the shit I have been through, even the Covid I contracted while writing these words here in isolation away from all my family and friends in Florida. I welcomed Covid into my body and the meaning I chose was so I could be incomplete isolation to finish this book. I could have chosen to believe it was unfair and why me and felt very sorry for myself. As my dear friend and mentor Tony Robbins often says life is happening for me, not to me.

When you can finally decide that you designed your whole life, the women, the failed marriages, the money, success, lack of happiness, the fall out with the children, people owing you money, the lot... only then can you do something to change it. You shift from being victim to victor. From being at effect to cause.

This is the ultimate life hack. It takes courage to say, 'Ok, I did this. I attracted the shit.'

When you can be brave enough to sit with that, this is the place we can start the magic. This is the place where we can turn the corner and you can really find a clear roadmap. Until now you have been going round and round in circles or burying your head in the sand and blaming others for putting you there. It is the harsh truth, gentlemen, but I know, believe and trust if you can swallow this pill then the gateway to a new road just opened for you and, boy, is this an exciting path.

The reason not many people go here and they live a life of misery is because the life of misery is all they know. It's comfortable. The only problem is that it is boring and predictable. Picture an uber wealthy man and wife in their seventies in the best restaurant money can buy, eating the best food and drinking the best champagne. Look at his face, the depth of his eyes, right into his soul and he is dead inside, and she is just going through the motions. That is someone who has settled for comfort. Nothing wrong with that if you want to have a mediocre life. A lot of people do. They have the money, the life and they convince themselves they 'should be happy' and this is what happiness is. They don't seek any more. **Dead in life,** I call this. They are usually bitter and very tight with their money because that is all they have control of. They seek control and comfort.

Nothing wrong with that unless you desire true happiness, excitement and fulfilment in life. There is a flip side to this and this is that you have to get uncomfortable and be ok with the unknown. Let me explain - imagine three circles - a small one then a medium size around the small one and then a bigger one outside of all the circles. Like a donut configuration. The centre circle is your comfort zone, the middle one is your uncomfortable zone and the outer one is your panic. If you stay in the comfort zone for most of your life, you will never change your life. You more or less live the same life as your parents. Nine to five job, they know when they are going to eat, what they are going to have each day of the week and at what time; they live a very predictable life.

This is not a life you have followed. You have a very different life from your parents and you craved adventure and growth. Here is where you have sat for most of your business career - in the uncomfortable zone. You have taken risks without any guarantees of the outcome. You have pushed and stepped into courage where no other man would go. As a result, you grew and so too did your comfort zone. The things that once terrified you in business are now the norm for you. Your comfort zone actually expanded, resulting in all your zones expanding. Your uncomfortable zone, your panic zone. So the things in the past that may have sent you into panic no longer send you into panic because they have become part of your comfort zone as the circles get bigger.

I remember when my hubby and I first got married. He started his business and he put all our assets on the line to get a loan. I thought he was crazy. I remember feeling sick and panicking, having cold sweats. I would have dreams of being homeless and living on the streets, hating him for putting a professional on the streets. What would I tell my patients? Where would I wash my clothes, all these thoughts! My brain went into overdrive. It was right on the edge of my uncomfortable zone and panic, but over the years this became a regular occurrence until it became part of what we do - my comfort zone.

We have experienced it so many times and I always have a roof over my head and somewhere to wash my clothes. It became comfortable. My comfort zone expanded and now it takes much bigger numbers for me to feel any discomfort. In fact, I have now mastered the art of living in the discomfort to the degree that when we went skydiving over The Palm in Dubai I actually felt no fear, just excitement. It was the first time I had ever skydived, but I realised something. I was at choice. I made a decision that today was an opportunity I wouldn't get every day. I could choose to enjoy the whole thing or be terrified of the worst case scenario. The memory I have will be with me forever, breathtaking! Have you ever had a moment in your life when you decided to go for it and enjoy it rather than fear it? Now, think about the memories you have as a result of that decision. What if you decided every moment could create magic memories?

How often in life do we face a terrifying moment that we chose to put ourselves in and then unconsciously experience the whole thing in fear? We allow our subconscious programming to take over and run the show. And then live to regret it?

I am so guilty of this. 95% of our thoughts and beliefs are subconscious and automatic. We don't even know they are running the show and often because of a seven-year-old that had one bad experience which was imprinted as the only roadmap for that experience for the rest of their lives. Let that land for a moment. We have allowed our seven-year-olds, particularly in the area of personal relationships, to run the show while we have been asleep for decades. It is no wonder that 50% of marriages end in divorce and fewer and fewer people are successful in life and relationships. We are all asleep and when we are awake for moments a seven year old brain is running the show! Madness!

It's time to wake up! I woke up that day on the sky dive. I decided that my scared four-year-old was not going to run the show, my grown arsed 40+ woman was. She was going to ask all the right safety questions and trust the guy with the pink glasses who had done five jumps a day for twenty years and she was going to enjoy the view from his office today. It was like a dream. One of the most magical experiences of my life!

All your beliefs are formed from the past, mostly from childhood, and that they may not be the best opinions to be running the show now. It might just be time for an upgrade. The definition of insanity is to keep doing what you are doing and expect different results.

What if today was the day you decided to think differently and take a chance with you and relationships and step into your uncomfortable zone and do something different? Trust? Trust you are safe. Trust you will be ok even if it doesn't work out the way you predicted. It might even work out better.

What if you decided today that you were no longer taking that highway to misery and you could see a new footpath that had always been there, you just never noticed it before. It looks a little rocky and not well-trodden but it's exciting because you don't know where it goes. Dare you get out of your comfort zone to try a new way?

What have you got to lose?

You know there are patterns forming some of the richest men in the world: Elon Musk, Bill Gates, Tony Robbins all divorced, not because they didn't provide enough money but because they didn't do this inner work I am talking about. The emotional intellect piece. They continued to do the same thing in their relationships - blame others, give little focus and attention, become pleasers, hand off their balls, speak like they were communicating with men. They didn't invest in finding out about themselves and all their beliefs and values. They assumed relationships come naturally and finally they did not educate themselves on the true meaning of happiness.

Were they successful? Hell, yes, but by whose definition? Are they happy? Does money buy it all for them? Yes, it gives us access to faster vehicles for that highway I was talking about. You get to travel that highway even faster and in as many different luxurious ways as possible. But what is the point if you are on the highway to lonely or miserable? Wouldn't you rather have joy and happiness walking the dirt path and noticing everything on the way, even if it was on your own?

This is the reason you F up so many times in this area of life. You are on the same highway going round and round in circles, in fast and fancier vehicles. GET OFF!

Take the slow path like you did in business right at the beginning and really invest in you and then learn about the opposite sex.

I am going to cover what women really want in the next chapter but before you jump into it, it is important you re-read this chapter. You will be tempted and I know 80% will not do this and some will even skim over this chapter to get the gold - what women really want. If you do listen to me and do the work in this chapter, you will be so much more effective in the next chapter. If you are still tempted to skip it, ask yourself this...

How many times in your life is it a familiar pattern for you where you cut corners and wonder why she is pissed with you? Remember, it's not about getting there but experiencing the journey along the way. Feeling every rock underfoot on that dirt path, hearing every bird, understanding how you relate to all of this. In the next chapter when I talk about how to make her happy, if you rush to the end you will completely miss the point. You may as well be back on the highway to hell, not the footpath to fulfilment.

So go back and read it again and get clear on what beliefs and values have been running your show. Are they true? And are they working for you? If not, what would you rather believe?

66

'WHEN THERE IS NOTHING LEFT
TO HIDE THERE IS NOTHING LEFT
TO SEEK.'

Ester Perel

10

WHAT DO WOMEN REALLY WANT?

This is the million, no... billion, dollar question. It's the No.1 question that men ask me. They think that if I give them this, all their problems will be solved and their lives will be amazing. They will be the wealthy stud muffin that is not only the envy of all his rich friends but also has the very happy and satisfied lady on his arm. He has it all! And to an extent this is true. However, it's not what they think it is and you guys love the idea of it but don't want to do the work to get there. You want the fast pass. If that was the case you would all have the dream and be bored out of your brains.

Let's first talk about the fact that men and women are different - I know, stating the bloody obvious. Yet we expect the opposite sex to want the same things and then get surprised when they don't. That is because we are different and also because our roles in society have changed.

Let's think about this: in the 1940s our grandparents had less confusion and there were few failed marriages. Men went to work and **provided** and the women **nurtured** the family. The roles were really simple and clear. Hence the term, the man is bringing home the bacon. This set up goes back centuries to caveman times when the women stayed in the tribe and the men went out to hunt. It worked.

Our brains have not evolved much in this area but the difference nowadays is that modern marriages no longer have these clearly defined roles, because women can now provide for themselves and men can pay for a maid to take care of them. So what is the point of modern day relationships? It is actually *LOVE*. Couples are entering relationships for love not to be provided for or nurtured. So the question is, if love conquers all, why is the divorce rate so high?

Here is the fundamental problem in all high value relationships. Are you ready for it? Nobody dares say it, but our reptilian brains still desires the old-fashioned values. Men still need to feel they are bringing home the bacon, women want to be provided for emotionally and with focus and attention, and men still want to feel taken care of. There is a battle between societal norms and pressures and biology. The problem is getting bigger and bigger the more money women make. Most wealthy self-made women still want to be cherished and taken care of by a man and most men want to be honoured and respected. This is just a little background to the evolution of relationships. It's a snapshot. There are so many other factors, like a lack of role models, but that's for another time.

Let's rewind a bit and set the context of this chapter. This chapter is placed here in the book because I know that many of you would have only read this one if it was at the beginning, right? Let's be honest. The problem with that is that it would have made sense on a cognitive level and you would have applied the information and wondered why she still wasn't happy. Here is why. I believe we learn information on three levels and it is only when we fully learn on all three levels does it become effective. Until then it will feel like you have read a book and are just going through the motions. A bit like a sex book - they can teach you all the moves and as a teenager it can work for you, but as you and your women gets more sophisticated the same moves will leave you both bored and wanting more.

The three levels are:

Level One: Cognitive

This when you know the information, like when you learn to drive a car. You know that the brakes will stop the car and the accelerator will make it go and that the gear stick will change the gears. So yes, you can technically drive, but it is a very functional, clunky driving experience.

Level Two: Heart Centred

This is when you have the knowledge, apply it and are able to use it intuitively. This is when your gut instinct is involved. Your drive effortlessly. You feel when to accelerate and you brake when you pull a corner. It's a very different experience from cognitive knowing.

Level Three: Embodiment of Knowledge

This is when you know and feel the information. Take the driving example - you are a very smooth driver, very safe, when you are in level two. Most people are happy living this level of understanding but high achievers like you don't settle for mediocre; you desire outstanding. That is this level. This is the answer to making a woman happy. If you can commit to learning all of this from a place of embodiment then you have nailed it. So what is embodied learning? It's when not only do you feel when to accelerate or brake but you and the car become one. You are a direct extension of the car. You become the knowledge. It becomes part of you. You become a man who effortlessly makes all women happy not by what he does but by who he has become when he is doing it. Just his presence alone is all she needs and she melts. Can you imagine having that kind of power? This is embodied knowledge. It's in your DNA.

In this chapter I am going to teach you the knowledge but at what level you choose to learn it is up to you and will ultimately determine your results.

The first thing a woman wants is not what you think - it is not sex, sorry to disappoint you. She loves sex but it has a very different definition to a woman especially a woman that you have been with for several years. If you get it right, the quality of your sex life will provide more than a physical connection.

Let me help you out here. Sex to a woman is not intercourse.

Sex for her starts not when you get a hard on but from the moment you open your eyes and you see her. When you notice the light on her skin and you touch her hair and stroke her forehead. When you linger in her presence not to have intercourse but because she is the most beautiful thing you have ever seen. She is the sexiest thing you have ever seen. Think about the feeling you get when you touch your dream car for the first time. It's that feeling.

It's not stroking her while checking your emails or trying to play a game one handed. She feels everything. Women are born with heightened senses. That is how she knows when you are lying. It's not what you say or do but who you are/be when you do it. So if you want a horny wife or you want to be the best lover, it starts with letting go of the possibility of having sex but being so fully present with her just because you can't resist her chemistry. By doing this you are letting her know she is the first and most important thing in your life, above your cell phone. This, when done properly (in level three), can take minutes but is so effective. Then you just get on with your day. No sex, remember it's the journey.

The next thing is, during the day send her text messages just saying heartfelt messages, not about what you want to do but how she makes you *feel*. Remember her currency is feeling not facts.

Now, gentleman, this is where the work really begins for you. For years men have been taught to suppress their feelings - 'Boys don't cry,' or 'Stop acting like a girl and man up.' Most men have never witnessed another grown man cry or had a role model to teach them how to express emotions other than anger and so all emotions have been mashed into anger. It was the only one they were allowed to express. Unfortunately, that has meant we have a nation of men who feel so desperately but don't know how to express it. Gentlemen, this is where the work is for you. It is a huge piece of work and a whole book in itself on how to fully feel and express those feelings without judging yourself. This is the work that I take my beautiful brave clients on as they finally meet themselves. It's magical.

Anyhow, let's get back on track. What women want.

The sex thing for us women starts not with you asking for it but you teasing us all day. Not with your sex moves, grabbing our boobs, bum, pushing your hard on next to our bodies, but with your attention. Like sweet text messages, anticipating our needs like opening the door for us or helping carry the heavy shopping. It's your typical chivalry moves. A gentle kiss for no reason. A stroke of the arch of her back as she brushes past you. Running her a bath but taking extra care to add rose petals and her favourite bath salts. Pouring her a nice glass of wine or making her favourite cup of tea, especially when she didn't ask.

Why do all these things matter? It's about the **effort** you put in, not what you **provide/buy**. This is one of the biggest mistakes men make. They keep buying things - bags, coats, holidays and cars - instead of giving her their presence with their attention. It's so sad and frustrating because a lot of money is wasted. You may as well just throw it down the toilet. In fact, give it to charity.

Let me explain. Yes, she loves all her gifts but not as a replacement for your efforts and attention. You might argue that a lot of effort went into making the money and it is true. However, she was not the sole reason for you making the money. She wants to feel that you give her something money can't buy and is one thing and one thing only. YOUR FOCUS. Undivided, level three presence. That is it.

Many of you are going to be so pissed reading this because you have spent a fortune and still felt like it wasn't good enough. The truth is, it's not that the things you provided weren't appreciated, they just weren't the thing that lights all women up. See it as a compliment that **she chose YOU to light her up**. Out of all the men, she believes **you are the one** that lights her up. When you can fully start to embody your power as a strong man, all you have to provide is your focus and presence to make her happy. (Even as I re-read this for my final edit this paragh gives me chills all over my body at the thought of my man's undivided attention and focus. now that's power). **It will save you so much ener**gy.

Here is what I want you to know about women. They don't mean what they say.

So if you have spent a lifetime giving a woman everything she says she wants, that is where you have been going wrong. I know it is confusing. I know it's mind blowing to think that we are not logical and clear in our requests. Why would we even bother asking for something if we don't actually want that thing? I know this is going to sound crazy, but we are testing your manhood all the time by seeing how you respond to our crazy demands. So how do you pass? Do you give her what she asks for? Or should you not? What is the test?

Sometimes you do and sometimes you don't, but you never give every time. 99% of you have lost the will to live at this point and I can totally understand, because it makes no logical sense. And you would be right, it doesn't. I will let you into a secret. It makes no sense whatsoever for us either. Let me give you an analogy. Imagine the woman is the ocean. She moves in an unpredictable way, with no logic. You never know when she will be calm and when suddenly there will be a storm. She can't tell you how long or in what direction the storm will be. This is Mother Nature. It makes no logical sense. Got the idea?

The next piece is to imagine the man is the ship navigating the waters. His job is to anticipate the waters - the calm and the storms. Every storm and weather front is unpredictable and different. The only thing the man can do is do his best to learn the lessons from conquering each storm allowing him to build his confidence in keeping the boat afloat. How does he do this? He plays the game. He does allow fear of the ocean to stand in his way. He takes his boat out to sea each time and the more he takes it out the more he learns how to navigate every storm until he becomes the master of the ocean. And each time he arrives home safely, he has grown. His comfort zone has grown because he dared to set sail and expand his comfort zone.

When she asks you for something or says something, use this example to help you decide whether you should take her at her word or not. In our tenth year of marriage I said something because money was tight. We had just had our second child and I was trying to ease the burden in my 'logical' brain and I said to my man, 'Don't buy me flowers - they are a waste of money.' He took me literally and didn't buy me flowers for ten years! I don't blame him but I bet if he had used his gut instinct he would have come to a very different conclusion. At that time neither of us understood the differences nor did we have the developed emotional intellect that we have now.

This is a prime example of why you never, never take a woman's word as gospel. We operate from feelings not facts.

(Head up: all women love flowers and if they tell you they don't listen beyond their words.)

As a man you are probably wondering why the hell God/the creator/whatever you believe in created such a complicated creature? I have asked myself this question so many times. It makes no sense and I even drive myself mad with my total illogicalness. Take this example. I am in Florida isolating, my man is in Dubai isolating, because we both got Covid one after another. We have been separated for ten days now after being together 24/7 for eight months. He started calling me and I was playing hard to get, but the minute he lost interest in the chase I started calling him and bugging him. It makes no logical sense even to me as the expert, but what I do realise is that this dance for attention is real.

I realise as a woman that we do it for attention and to keep the mystery. It's like we leave clues for you to solve like a detective. I realise that the reasons we are not straight forward are:

1. It would be very boring for everyone if life was predictable.
2. The unpredictability that a woman provides with you gives you the capacity to grow, to learn how to navigate that boat in the crazy ocean.
3. It provides you with an opportunity to test your strength and grounding. Can you withstand the storm and know it is not about you but that it is just Mother Nature?

One thing that an immature man does repeatedly in this situation is that he sinks his boat. It is not for the want of trying to hold the boat against the toughest storms. It is actually because when he allows the water on his ship and he internalises the storm as a direct attack on him, he is then doomed, the boat fills with water and he eventually capsizes and becomes the storm. He becomes feminised and demasculated. Why? Because he hasn't done the inner work on himself to know that the storm has nothing to do with him and everything to do with his woman. His only job is to navigate, learn and grow from the storm.

As women we say some horrific things. It doesn't make it right. In fact, it is very wrong, very wrong, but we do it for two reasons:

1. We are scared.
2. We are testing whether you (the man) will save me from the worst enemy of all - myself.

The fear is not about the big bad wolf. We know there is no imminent danger. We just have an internal battle with our own internal storm and all the sea dragons that live in the ocean. We test you to see if you are man enough to stand firm and know that all the verbal diarrhoea is not directed at you (even though the words coming out of her mouth sound like they are). Get beyond the feeling that it is an attack on you but understand that it is a sign she needs rescuing. Now that is mastering the woman.

Guys, if you can master this, you will own your woman. She will not go anywhere else. In the next chapter I will explain why this is very rare, how difficult it is for men to achieve and what it takes to achieve it.

There is a lot in this chapter so let me summarise it:

1. The words she uses are not what she means; her world is feelings not facts.
2. It's who you are, not what you do. Remember she can smell a fake.
3. If you can look beyond the attack then you will go from being a hacked man to her hero.

So you can see why women are so complex. Sorry, gentlemen, but not sorry, because the more complex we are in life, the more passionate and wild we are in bed. It is worth it to figure this one out.

In the next chapter I am going to talk about why very few men never achieve hero status. If you can recognise this in yourself then you can change it. Simple.

66

"MAN IS NOTHING ELSE
BUT WHAT HE MAKES OF
HIMSELF."

Jean-Paul Sartre

11

ADDICTION TO PLEASING

T his chapter is going to trigger you, which is why I have left it to the end. By now you know I am not a yes girl, but a truth girl. I was talking to a client and they said, 'Just tell me as it is, Dimple. If I can't take it, I will get over it.' I am not here to be liked. I am here for you to get results and win at life and love.

Let's take a moment to assess what I mean by being a 'pleaser' and why this triggers most men in your position.

The first way I define a pleaser: It's a man who constantly says yes to his partner's every request even if he knows it is completely the wrong thing. He gets into a habit of having the quick solution and dopamine rush rather than being truthful to what she needs rather than wants. This subject triggers most emasculated men because deep in your subconscious mind you have known for a long time you have given in to pleasing and pacifying her for a quiet life.

If you can't take it, you need to learn *why not* and *what you must do to get over it.* What is it inside of you that is causing this anger/shame/guilt? This is the work, my friends. Yes, this is the chapter for you! Hard core, straight-talking facts aiming for massive growth and expansion for you.

It is going to hit some home truths. I have spent chapters nurturing you and now it is time to take the velvet glove off to reveal the iron fist.

It is time to tell you what you need to hear not what you want. The question is: *Are you man enough to take it?*

Now remember, everything I say comes from a place of love and courage. This is not because I am a man basher - though I have been very guilty of this in the past.

First I want you to brace yourself and take a **deep breath.** I mean it, do it.

There is a reason why I ask you to breathe: it **gets you out of your f**king head** and helps you feel my intention. That is to help you, find **YOU** again. You know, the man who wears his 'balls' with pride in his relationship. The one who knows how to give his woman what she needs not what she wants or asks for.

This is exactly my intention for this chapter and is behind the reason men lie to their wives.

I have realised that in this century there is a growing number - 80% - of men who have been raised by women with no or very few strong male role models. As a result we have a nation of 'pleaser' men who would rather be 'yes' men and go against their gut and lose themselves in order to have a peaceful life. They have spent a lifetime being taught by strong masculine women to be 'good' boys and gentlemen and taught how to please their mummies, sisters and, frankly, most women.

Ok, so now I have set the scene and you are clear on my intention to serve you, I will explain my theory.

The reason this conversation is coming up now is because of a clubhouse room. I was asked to be an expert speaker. It became very clear that men, not just young men but older men in power, were still 'victims' too.

The plague of *'the mummy's boy'* otherwise known as the *'the pleaser plague'*.

Yes, the syndrome of fear of upsetting the women.

This doesn't mean I am blaming your mothers nor you, because you were both unconscious of the damage you were doing. In fact, she was doing what she thought was the right thing by you in her frame of the world, with all the hurt she had endured with men.

It's this very same thing that is the reason boys in China are being sent to masculinity school. The curse of *'the mummy's boy.'* Protect and provide for the little darlings so they can't get hurt. Wrap them up in cotton wool. Don't allow them to fall. *'Oh, be careful, darling!'*

How often have you heard that growing up or heard a mother say it to their little boy?

I am not bashing mothers - I happen to be one. The reason I am being so abrupt is to let you know we (women) are not as fragile as you think. We protect and provide for our children like fierce lionesses and that's why we jump to the rescue.

The problem is not the lioness but the rise in the lioness being the sole parent and boys being raised by single mothers. They don't have the balance of the masculine role - the father who lets him climb the tree, fall, and then brush himself off.

The father is not fearful of telling his wife the truth about how she looks in the dress, not to be mean but because he respects himself enough to know that if she can trust him to tell the truth, even if she doesn't like it, then she can trust him to keep her safe. Her job is to be self-aware enough not to need reassurance from him about her body and to be strong enough to want the truth. After all, nobody wants to be seen with a woman in a dress that looks bloody awful and she certainly doesn't want to look like a dog's dinner either. She should trust her man enough to know he loves her enough to never let that happen.

So why do men lie about these things? Surely honesty is the best way?

Here is the golden gem. The one thing that once men overcome it, they will not only have their woman look amazing but also think he is amazing!

The reason men can't say when she asks, 'Do I look fat in this?' ... 'Yes, dear, you do,' (if she does) is because of 'fear' of upsetting first their mothers and now their wives. They have been conditioned from a young age not to upset their single mother (or if their father works away or is absent emotionally - a whole other story to dig into) because they run the risk of being abandoned (physically and or emotionally). therefore not worthy of love.

Men are punished for upsetting their mothers and wives if they speak their truth. They are left feeling very hurt and confused. Their mothers scold them or withhold love and affection and their wives withhold sex and connection. It is brutal. That is a woman's way of keeping control/power, having the upper hand. Putting him in his place. What this does to the men is that it programmes them to seek love and affection, acceptance through pleasing, even at the cost of losing themselves. The reason women do it is because we are generally physically smaller than men and so the only way we can control men is to withhold affection and connection. Most women are completely oblivious to the damage they are causing to men, in a bid to protect themselves.

The challenge here is for you, gentlemen. If you have never been taught how to speak your truth while still reassuring her, then you will find yourself being demasculated time and time again... **handing over your 'balls' on a silver platter.**

I see this over and over again. Let me summarise the problem.

1. Lack of strong male roles growing up.
2. Being overprotected as a child.
3. Women wanting reassurance from you but not asking you directly for it and are unable to find it in themselves.
4. You have never been taught it is ok to speak your truth even if it means she will be hurt - she is stronger than you think.
5. Women trying to keep you small by withholding affection.

So *what is the solution?*

Well, it is very simple.

Reclaim your balls.

This takes courage. This takes you to be willing to face rejection and abandonment and trust that you are man enough to deal with this. You are not broken. You will be ok. In fact, it is a knowing that not only will you be ok but you will grow from this, reclaiming your manhood and strength.

And the added bonus is that your woman will love you more for it because she can trust you to tell the truth. Translated for her, this means safety. If you can deal with her upset by being a man and speaking your truth then she can trust you to protect her from the sabretooth tiger.

This is what I like to call win, win, win!

A win for you (the man), win for her (the woman), and win for all because you now become the role model for all the men and boys you come into contact with. A safer and happier place for all our children collectively.

It is in these very conversations and of course, navigating the exact language on how you manage the whole 'do I look fat in this dress?' conversation that I coach my elite executives who earn 8/9 figures.

So please don't think successful men don't suffer from the plague. They do. They have just decided to take a different roadmap on how to reclaim their manhood. Finding themselves again.

Now before I move on to the final chapter, I want to briefly touch on a pandemic of men who have a history of ending relationships for no good reason. They find themselves sabotaging themselves. Picture this: a fifty-year-old man, super successful, married for twenty years and has two grown up children. Everything looks perfect on the outside, and suddenly he leaves for no real reason.

Or he is a man in his fifties who has spent his whole life in and out of amazing relationships and just when it starts to get too good to be true, he ends it and leaves. If this is you or you know someone who is like this, you are possibly asking *why the hell does he do that?* He has got exactly what he desires, a woman who loves him and is fun to be around, is committed to him and not his money. Yet he ups and leaves. I knew one man who did this three times with the same lady. She was devastated.

You get the picture. It is all linked to abandonment or should I say, fear of abandonment. It is the reason men become pleasers. Let's unpack this for you because once you are aware, you can do something about it. You can start to take radical responsibility for your actions.

A man who fears abandonment stemming from two places - childhood or ancestral - will sabotage the possibility of anyone abandoning him. The thought of someone leaving him is more painful than him taking control and leaving her first.

Less painful to be the abandoner than the abandoned.

Let that land. The thought of the pain of being left (even if that is very unlikely to happen) is worse than ending a perfectly good relationship. He will end it before she does, even if she was never going to. Something kicks in his head and a safety mechanism takes over. It makes no sense whatsoever, but as humans we will move away from the biggest perceived pain. In this case it is the *thought* of being abandoned and so the sabotage that actually leaves you alone and heartbroken is safer because it wasn't in the control of a woman. This is how many men try to reclaim their manhood and power. There is just one problem with it: they never reclaim their manhood, they just avoid it by running away and avoid manning up to the fear of abandonment. They put a plaster or bandaid on the wound but never address the wound. And the wound heals on the surface and they move on to the next relationship until that gets too good to be true. Sirens go off in their brain: danger, danger, possible abandonment may occur because the heart is getting too close. It will hurt big time; better leave now to avoid that nasty pain. Bandaid is ripped off and the wound is wide open again and never heals.

So what's the solution, I hear you ask? *This is me all over,* I hear you screaming at the book. How do I fix it? Use my five step model that I am going to share with you. It is simple and effective and requires real courage. Transformation is easy but it requires guts and courage, hence only 1% of the population of men in particular ever go there. Congratulations: the fact that you are reading this book means you are part of that 1%.

This model is aptly called The Heart Model. It was developed one day when I was preparing for an international speaking engagement in NYC and has been proved very successful at providing men with clarity on their goals in all areas of life. So here it is:

H – onesty; this is the most painful part. Be honest with yourself and admit, yes I have been the problem, not the circumstances, the kids, the wife or the girlfriend and don't make it bigger or smaller than what it is, but just as it is. Write it down and state it loud and clear, not shaming or guilting yourself but just the facts. When you look at it like this, you can do something about it, because you then look at the *real* problem, not the BS you have been hiding behind for years. Let's use the analogy of your business. The worst thing you can do when your business is heading south is to fix it on false numbers or should I say creative BS numbers. It's never going to be successful. So do a truthful audit and take responsibility for it.

E – ducation Now you know the truth and what you are dealing with, get an education - a book, a mentor, a coach you respect that has the results you want. Let's look at business. If there was something that needed fixing would you roll up your shelves and fix it? Or would you hire an accountant or finance expert? Or if there was a litigation problem, who you decide it was time to start becoming a lawyer? NO, it would be dangerous because you don't know this subject. It takes years to become an expert in that field and so you pay for the years of investment they have made in that area and their years of experience. You are paying for the fast pass. So why is it in the area of life that matters the most - the part that is responsible for our happiness - we think we can fix it ourselves? Maybe you can. Or you may spend a lifetime trying and never achieve it. Short answer: GET a COACH if you want the fast pass just like you would in business. Hire the best, you don't want to screw up this part of your life because it kinda has a knock on effect everywhere else.

A - rticulate your truth. Learn how to speak it in a way that doesn't make anyone lose. This is the one area in life where you don't want a winner and loser. If they lose, you lose. The relationship loses. Learning how to communicate your needs in a way that is not only masterful but respectful is key to you successfully reclaiming your manhood and identity. Stop saying nothing and learn to say it with love and respect, not to win but to do the right thing.

R - esolve your differences. Decide that the past is the past and how you, she, they behaved was then. Decide to stop reliving the past. The moment we decide to stop living in the past is the moment we stop living the past over and over. Think about it in business - do you keep doing the same thing and expecting people to respond the same way because they made a mistake in the past? No, you give people and yourself the benefit of the doubt, you give them a second chance or you fire them. Yet in relationships we always believe they will do the same and will respond in the same way and then guess what happens? We expect the past and sure enough we get exactly that! No wonder, you just called it in. At this stage it is all about moving on. Forgive yourself for the past and learn what you needed to learn and move on! Move on and start getting excited about new possibilities and watch what magic you attract.

T - ry new things - test the waters. The definition of insanity is doing the same thing over and over again and expecting different results. This is like going to an accountant and getting the advice you need to solve a problem and then doing nothing different! Madness. Yet we all do it when it comes to matters of the heart and love. We do this because matters of the heart are the most painful to deal with if we fail. The fear of failing in this area becomes so overwhelming that we just go back to our default and go for the easy life and become complacent and fatigued. So the key to this step is - Stop it! Face your fear and do it anyway - you have nothing to lose but everything to gain. You might say that you could end up divorced and I would say, yes this is true. But what would you be divorcing from? A marriage that is already dead. It would give you peace and freedom in the long run, or you could actually heal your marriage and experience freedom and peace with the one you love? I know which one I would rather have!

For those of you that want to understand this model more I have an online program on this for purchase at www.dimple-global.com. Go check it out.

66

'A MAN CANNOT BE
COMFORTABLE WITHOUT
HIS OWN APPROVAL.'

Mark Twain

12

THE BONUS - HOW TO GAIN CONFIDENCE WITH POWERFUL WOMEN

You know by now I want you to win. I want you to have your roadmap to success so I decided to throw in a bonus chapter. This will help you understand why and what happens when you lose your confidence with powerful women and the impact on the women. You will learn my five step strategy on how to gain confidence with women. So here it is:

I was moderating a Clubhouse room a couple of weeks ago on 'conscious confidence' and it became very apparent that lack of confidence is not just a female thing.

In fact, when I look back over the decades of coaching men I realise that their *confidence, self-esteem, and self-worth* have taken a hammering over the years.

Now, you may say this is no different from women and you would be correct. The only difference here is that men are not taught or encouraged to deal with it on a daily basis. In fact, the opposite occurs: they are shamed or guilted into not dealing with it and **brush it under the carpet.**

Women are encouraged to talk and articulate their emotions from a very young age using over two thirds more words than men in a day. Men are told from a very young age that boys don't cry. *Stop shouting. Be quiet. Stop being a cry baby.* **Man up!**

All words that over time require their brains and neurology to bury feelings. To not only not feel but to not express feelings. They are taught to dampen down the sounds they use as boys to express the full rainbow of feelings from joy to anger and rage.

It is no wonder that man suicide is so prevalent. According to the charity, The Samaritans, 25.5% of suicides are of men aged 45-49 compared with 7.4% of suicides being women of the same age.

Boys and men are being taught to suppress feelings, not release them and when those feelings do bubble to the surface to feel guilt and shame for doing so! This cycle is passed down from generation to generation and the rise in male depression and mental health continues to increase.

This provides you with a little background as to why men lack confidence in general and now I want to move to why and how to address this problem, resulting in men feeling more confident in themselves and then with women.

Before I do, here is why you being more confident is actually going to get you the girl or pull the wife in. It's a little secret that the ladies know and I am going to let you in.

Do you want to know what women desire more than anything else?

A confident man. A man who makes the decisions, who leads even if it is not the way she would do it!

I know you are thinking, **'WHAT!'**

It is the biggest turn-on for women when a man takes control. Not in an, 'I am the man and you are the woman' caveman way but more like a quiet assertiveness. The energy of knowingness and strength. Think of how James Bond presents himself when he walks into the room.

Why does she desire and get turned on by this?

The number one human need women are magnetised to, yes magnetised to, is safety and security. When a woman feels that a man can make the difficult decisions and that he can **follow through** with absolute conviction, then she can fully trust him. When she can trust him, then she can 'let go'. She no longer needs to protect herself. She can drop into her femininity and be the girly, sexy, powerful temptress that you desire.

She can only do this with a confident man. *Why?* Trust! She has to be able to trust your word is gold!

So, think back to past relationships or even current ones where you have made a decision and she has said, 'No I don't want to do that,' and you back down even though you know in your gut that your decision was the right one? And at a later date, she comes back to you and says you were right.

Here's what happens in that - you make a decision (lacking conviction and therefore confidence), she tests your conviction and says she wants to do something else and you back down because you want to make her happy. For example:

Woman: Where do you want to go for dinner?

Man: I will take care of it, leave it to me.

Woman: Ok.

Thirty seconds later...

Woman: I think we should go to The Savoy. Yes, I will book it.'

The man sighs: Ok - ✖ (Not the response she wants.)

The man: Thank you for the suggestion. I will take care of dinner.. ✅ (The response she wants.)

I know this is a silly example, but *doesn't it always start like this?* Here's why it is a problem to not follow through with your promises. She now believes that you are not a man of your word and she can't trust you with a small decision so *how can she trust you to keep her safe?*

I know you are thinking that *she* asked to do something different! Yes, she did but women don't mean what they say, they feel what they mean. She is testing whether, when you are faced with an obstacle, you rise up or back down.

Can she trust you if the sabretooth tiger starts to attack? Will you be man enough to rise and fight him or will she get eaten as you run away?

This is what is going on in her subconscious. She probably has no idea that she is testing you or why she is testing you. All the while you just want to please her, make her happy and give her what she wants and asks for. Like if she wants to eat at The Savoy - you are ok with that, but she is testing, can she trust you to organise it and follow through?

The logical part of you right now is mind-blown. I know. I covered why she does this in the communication chapter. For now, understand that what she wants is for you to honour your word with confidence especially when she tests. Even when she resists your decision.

Ok, so that is the why for your relationships now let's look at why confidence is so important for YOU.

Every time you have an experience where you feel a lack of confidence, you gather evidence that you are not good at it. It feels painful and as humans, we are designed to move away from pain. You start to develop a highway of neurons to avoid situations that require confidence and you have a whole library of evidence as to why the no-confidence highway is a safer option. In the meantime, the highway to confidence and the library of evidence that you are confident starts to diminish. You end up with a dirt track to confidence and zero books in that library. This is all going on in your nervous system and you are completely unaware of it.

Over the years you become comfortable with the avoidance highway so much so that it becomes who you are and you start saying, '*I am terrible with women*' or '*I have no confidence*' or '*I am not confident.*'

The moment you shift from a lack of confidence as a behaviour to your identity - this is when you enter the danger zone. It is very difficult to shift identity... but not impossible.

So here is how:

1. Notice your self-talk - how often do you say *I am not confident?* Catch yourself and start to reprogram the language you use: e.g. *Up until now I wasn't confident* or *I need to practice confidence in this area.*

2. Start to gather evidence of other areas in your life where you were confident. Being aware means you can start to fill those empty shelves in your library of evidence for confidence. The mind doesn't need to

know which situation you were confident in. Just
that you have evidence of being confident.

3. Notice when you lack confidence and be aware of
   where you feel it in your body. All you do is close
   your eyes and locate the pain. Once you have it just
   feel it. Don't make it a big thing or add a story or a
   meaning to it. Feelings are just energy moving
   through our bodies. This is why we say 'feel the pain'
   in the gym. You have to tear the muscle to grow
   stronger. It will be uncomfortable. Remember,
   humans are designed to move away from pain. Stick
   with it, your job is just to feel it, cry, scream , do what
   you need to and it will pass.

4. When it passes, continue to do the thing or make the
   decision that you were going to move away from
   before. Pain is a guide - it's time to grow.

5. Repeat and rise over and over again until the
   avoidance highway becomes a dirt path and has
   empty shelves in the library and the confidence dirt
   path is a highway to happy confident you and the
   women you are with.

This is my very brief five step strategy to kicking lack of confidence in the balls!

'CHOOSE LOVE OVER BEING RIGHT.'

Dimple Thakrar

13

SO WHAT NOW?

W ell, this is the end of this road for us and it's been wild. We have covered every turn and twist of the dirt track road. In this chapter before we part, I want you to know you are honoured and respected, you are worthy of love and your desire for connection is real.

It is unfortunate that men in today's society have been dealt a rough card. You are expected to provide and protect and every cell in your body desires that and yet women leave a very mixed signal. For years you do the right thing, you provide and protect and it doesn't feel enough. She always wants more.

I was listening to a very famous music director in LA (a dear friend of mine) and he described a story of his mother and step-father. This couple had been together for thirty years, the man providing everything so his mother didn't have to work. Bringing home $200,000 a month. They had the life, but it took him working many jobs. This man at seventy years old decided to retire, bringing their take home monthly to $200 a month. A drastic reduction, he was happy and tired and was content with providing for thirty years.

You would think the wife would be content, but according to my friend, (remember this is his mother) she complained that her husband was lazy and he needed to get back out earning and that he would have to find a place of his own if he didn't go get a job and bring home more money. Now this man has given thirty years of his life and resulted in very little appreciation. He was weary and tired. I tell this story because I want you to notice who you think is the cause of this situation. The step-father or the wife?

I bet most of you will blame the wife. Nobody is to blame but the person who can fix it is the tired, weary man. It is this exact scenario that is happening in all households across the world, from high-influence people like the Gates and Elon Musk to regular people in the street. You see it everywhere, it is rife and so sad. It is the reason I wrote this book. Gentleman, I hope that in reading this book you can see why it is your responsibility to step up. To not ignore your gut instinct and speak your truth for you, for her and for the greater good of all. Enabling you to become the role model for the next generation. Here is why this is so important.

Yesterday I was a speaker at an event and a lady came on the stage. She is a massive influencer, empowering women to achieve financial independence. She came on the stage and said, 'Women don't need men.' She then went on to say that discussions with her 24-year-old left him very confused because where does that leave him if women don't need a man. Now these are the thought leaders influencing women to be independent - nothing wrong with financial independence but when you start to mix up the frequency of love and money and believe that money is where the power is, that is when there is a problem.

They are the only role models for these young men, as most are raised by single mothers. These mothers have experienced heartbreak at the 'blame' of men. They are not the ideal person to be influencing healthy men. Whether we like it or not, we have here two examples of why men are lost and women are rising in their inauthentic masculine. Now this would all be perfectly amazing if everyone was happy, but I know for a fact that at least 80% of the women in the ladies community (and I am talking 100,000 women) are not happy in love and are desperate to find a strong man to cherish them including the leader herself.

These stories are not to bash anyone. Everyone is doing the best job they can and the leader of the women's organisation is doing incredible things to get women out of poverty. The point of this conversation here is to say, gentlemen, wake up!

This is real, you are responsible for going through a twenty-year marriage only to find that she has moved on and all the time and money you put into that could be wasted, and the worst thing is you lose you in the process. This to me is a tragedy when it can all be fixed by you. I can understand in the past you didn't have the knowledge but now it is time to be your own superhero. When you save you first. When you decide that the pull and addiction to pleasing no longer serves you or her in the long term and you get off the highway to hell and walk the slow but very rewarding dirt track to heaven. Here is what happens - that very same dirt path suddenly gets walked more. Men start to follow you. The path becomes more visible because it becomes more of a path rather than a dirt path. Other men start to get curious and want to know that there is an alternative to the highway, they just haven't seen it or have been too afraid to go first.

Now let me tell you, walking this path comes with a hazard warning. You may lose the love of your life sooner than twenty years in and you may gain your self-respect in the process. This is the worst case scenario. The best scenario is your beloved stops wearing the trousers in the relationship because she can finally let go because you have taken charge and she feels safe. And because you start to lead the way at first there will be a storm because she is not used to it and it is very uncomfortable for her. Also, she is testing you. Are you sure you will lead? Can she trust you to protect her from the sabre-tooth tiger inside of her? There will be some transition time for you and her. Don't worry if you slip back, we all do. These are programs that have run in your body for decades and probably your ancestors. Just catch it and turn around and get back on the dirt track. It was just a slight detour. It's all good. You have got this. Look yourself in the mirror daily and state,

> **'I am a strong man who is worthy of love and can protect and provide for me and my family. I trust my gut instinct to be my barometer and navigation. I will always honour it and respond to it. I am a warrior, my own superhero. I lead the way for me first, then her and then all.'**

I activated this mantra with energy of science wisdom. For those of you who don't know I am an energy healer and alchemist. I transmute energy and old beliefs in minutes into new empowering beliefs. Many people come to me with ailments, pains in their bodies for which they have had no cure for years, decades and I lift them in just a few hours. The words in this book, especially this mantra, have all been downloaded from ancient wisdom and times and translated in a way that will be understood especially for you the readier. 90% of this book was channelled at 4am when spirit woke me up and said *write!*

I share this because I know that if you are reading this then you are chosen to read this transmission. It is meant for you because the universe has decided that you have the strength to change the paradigm. It is time for men to reclaim their power not in an immature way but in a leadership way. The embodiment of healthy masculinity where you have the confidence to be YOU unapologetically for the greater good of yourself first, your lady and then everyone else. Gentlemen all you have to do is keep moving forward, one step at a time. The more you do that, the more you will start to witness other men and couples comment. Some will be triggered, especially the women, but the men secretly inside will be like *yes this feels right.* How does he have the courage to keep his family in order without fearing abandonment? Now that is when the magic really brings happiness.

So what's next for you? You have all this knowledge and insight. Where do you want to go from here? Some of you will feel that this was a lot and is enough. Some of you will feel you want to understand more and continue the path with me. You can do this several ways.

Linkedin, Instagram, and facebook at Dimple Thakrar and I have my paid courses and coaching. So at the very least you should join my social media for the hours of free content.

To work with me one to one is application only via my website www.dimpleglobal.com

Just to be clear, the main men I work one to one with are multi-millionaires who are looking to improve their relationship skills and get really clear on their purpose in life. We co-create their bespoke roadmap to purpose, through achieving the impossible in nano time. How? Because I use quantum physics, strategy and energy to lift limiting beliefs and move you at a pace that will feel like a miracle.

Some of the results we have achieved:

- in three sessions my client goes from only speaking to his ex-wife via lawyers for five years to spending Christmas dinner with her and having a beautiful friendship
- saving over $500,000 in avoiding bad decisions
- men magnetising their dream business deal, home and lover in just three months.
- lifting debilitating stomach problems and anxiety in one session. Completely removing physical ailments that have plagued them for decades.
- removing a 15 year bed binding back pain in 45 mins resulting in them going from bed to walking again.

These are just a few ways I help my clients align to the next level of their lives, by eliminating stress and anxiety and providing real freedom and success. If this sounds like something you desire then I would be excited to consider your application. It is an application. Not everyone is ready to fly but for those that are it's magic!

I hate goodbyes and I will leave you with a funny story. Last month my hubby and I had to say goodbye to our elder daughter as we were going home. She lives alone in NYC and about a day before we left my hubby started to pick a fight over nothing. So they parted after having had a fight.

Then a week later he had to leave for Dubai and I was supposed to go with him, but unfortunately I tested positive for Covid and had to stay in Florida. He picked a fight with me again just as we were saying goodbye.

Anyhow I didn't think anything of it until our younger daughter rang me. She was in Dubai with her father and she was about to leave to go back home to the UK and her father had started picking a fight with her. I thought this *was interesting*. Every time he is about to leave his loved one he picks a fight for no reason. I mean my fight with him was because we didn't have enough suitcases. I had a problem that we could fix easily but he preferred to get angry about it. I sat and reflected on this. (My poor husband is my guinea pig.) I asked these questions -

Why does he always pick a fight just as he is about to leave someone?

What emotion is he trying to avoid?

As I said before men have only been taught to express anger, so if he picks a fight then he only has to feel anger and he gets to avoid sadness and sorrow.

Maybe he was picking a fight to avoid feeling sad?

I share this theory with you as we say goodbye just in case you are feeling any sorrow or any emotion. All of it is ok. Feel it all, gentlemen. Don't make a story about it. It is what it is and it will be ok.

On that note, God bless you and take care of yourself and if it feels right leave a review, share or gift another man this book today.

With much love and respect,

Dimple x

P.S I believe in you, and I know only you can be your own superhero!

I appreciate all your efforts and energy used to be the 1% that wants more!

Printed in Great Britain
by Amazon

82764383R00112